A N T O N

—THE—

DOVE FANCIER

And Other Tales of the Holocaust

BERNARD GOTFRYD

WASHINGTON SQUARE PRESS
PUBLISHED BY POCKET BOOKS

New York London Toronto Sydney Tokyo Singapore

"The Wedding Picture," "Mr. G.," "The Last Morning," "Anton the Dove Fancier," "Three Eggs," and "The Execution" first appeared in *Midstream* in slightly different form.

A WASHINGTON SQUARE PRESS *Original* Publication

A Washington Square Press publication of
POCKET BOOKS, a division of Simon & Schuster Inc.
1230 Avenue of the Americas, New York, NY 10020

Copyright © 1990 by Bernard Gotfryd

Gotfryd, Bernard.
    Anton, the dove fancier : and other tales of the Holocaust /
Bernard Gotfryd.
        p.   cm.
    ISBN 0-671-69137-6 :
    1. Holocaust, Jewish (1939–1945)—Poland—Fiction. 2.
World War, 1939–1945—Poland—Fiction. 3. Radom (Radom,
Poland)—Fiction. 4. Holocaust survivors—Fiction. I. Title.
PS3557.O7935A58 1990
813'.54—dc20   90-30504
                                                                     CIP

Printed in the U.S.A.

Acclaim for Bernard Gotfryd's

A N T O N
———THE———
DOVE FANCIER

"These are lovely, artless, and at times heartbreaking tales of a lost world. Even when dealing with the unthinkable horror of the Holocaust, Bernard Gotfryd never loses his faith in people or his love for them. A testament that the soul as well as the body can be healed."

—Howard Fast

"They are simple, lucid, and moving—vignettes of the agony of our times. I commend them as worthy of consideration. . . . "

—Irving Howe

"These stories are exquisite and heartbreaking. I thought of Primo Levi. Singer. Also Chekhov. . . . It's as if certain gestures and spoken words from a terrible time had been crystallized in Bernard Gotfryd's memory, waiting to be printed unforgettably on the minds of his readers."

—Eleanor Munro

"Bernard Gotfryd's sharing these precious memories with us is a generous gift indeed, and deserves our warmest thanks."

—E. J. Kahn, Jr.

"A tender, heartbreaking collage by a witness who has managed to capture the small moments and humor of his lost childhood, as well as the larger horror."

—Betty J. Lifton

"A new and important writer. . . . These stories are so true, so simple, and so clean that they are bound to last."

—Stephen Vizinczey

"Wonderful stories by a courageous and skillful writer."

—Ian Frazier

*To the memory of my parents, my relatives,
and the millions of innocent victims
of an unprecedented genocide, 1939–1945.*

Acknowledgments

I would like to extend my thanks for the encouragement I received while writing this book to Gloria and Stephen, Gina, Howard, Anders, Peter, Amy, Alex, and Ted, and my special appreciation to Ellie, David, and Mary-Ann.

Last but not least, I am grateful to my indefatigable literary agent, Julian Bach, who didn't give up, and to my forbearing editor, Stacy Schiff, for her enthusiasm and total dedication.

But above all, my gratitude goes out to the memory of Primo Levi, who inspired me to continue.

"Quo Vadis Domine?"

—Henryk Sienkiewicz

Contents

Introduction

I have wanted to tell my story for the longest time—for more than forty years, in fact. I have always been concerned that if I didn't set these moments down on paper I would forget them, but when I started to write I realized that one doesn't forget such tragic events, not even after forty years.

I can still hear my mother, hours before she was deported, begging me to go into hiding, begging me to survive to tell the world what the Nazis did to us. Her words have sat heavily on my mind; I lived with them, I shared them over and over with my children, with my friends, and with anybody who was willing to listen.

Very often processions of long-gone faces appear in my dreams, and the echoes from the ghettos and camps still reverberate in my ears.

Having worked as a photographer a better part of my life, I have had countless opportunities to meet personalities in the Arts and Letters. Upon finding out about my experiences under the Nazis many of these individuals urged me to write about my life. It was my duty to tell my story, they insisted; I owed it to my people.

The episodes I have chosen to write are about people, some flawed, some good, some evil. More importantly, they are about suffering and the endurance of the human spirit.

A N T O N
THE
DOVE FANCIER

THEFT OF A
TABLE

I must have been seven, going on eight. That summer my parents rented a cottage on a farm not far from the city of Radom, where we lived; we shared the small cottage with the farmer's family. Our half had a veranda, which our landlord had built for us. His family stayed in a large kitchen that also served as a dining area; above it was a sleeping loft for his children.

Mr. Joseph, our landlord, was a hardworking, quiet man whose mustache resembled that of Marshal Pilsudski, then the head of the Polish state. He was a well-built man of medium height with a ruddy face. He never wore shoes, even when it rained, and his feet were covered with crusty, dried mud. He was a man of a few words; in fact, I never heard him speak except to ask for something or to scold his children. His wife was a tall, skinny, cheerful woman, eternally busy, always on the run. She dressed simply, usually in a full skirt of some floral pattern and a white linen blouse, with a red kerchief over her head. Her bare feet were covered with cuts and bruises. They had three daughters and a son who was my age, and who was to be my playmate. During the week they all worked on

1

the farm from dawn to dusk. On Sundays we would see the whole family, dressed in their best, walking to church in an adjoining village. On this day they carried shoes in their hands, so as not to wear them out prematurely.

Our cottage stood at the edge of a meadow beside a gully with a cold brook running through it. The brook served as a refrigerator where we stored perishable foods inside big clay pots, tightly covered and protected by heavy rocks. To the right of our veranda was a flower and vegetable garden; past the garden was a ditch and a narrow cobblestone road with soft, sandy shoulders. A short distance behind the cottage one crossed a tiny makeshift bridge made of loosely connected wooden logs. At the other side stood a barn with double doors and a thatched roof; next to it stood the stable, a massive building reinforced by heavy beams. Flocks of starlings nested everywhere. Fields of wheat, barley, and potatoes stretched toward a shallow stream that flowed slowly through green pastures; beyond lay the forest, rich in wild berries of every kind, the rarest mushrooms, hazelnuts, and wildflowers. At one point around the bend the stream widened, creating a pool deep enough for swimming. It smelled of freshly cut hay and of pine trees. High up in the crowns of the trees storks built their nests, calling out with loud clacking sounds when they circled overhead.

My parents decided that this was an ideal place for children; my brother, sister, and I were to stay on the farm all summer with our grandmother, who was to take care of us while our parents returned to the family business in Radom. Grandmother was a diminutive lady. She covered her head with a kerchief during the week; on holidays the kerchief gave way to a wig. Then one could find her next to the kitchen window, where the light was good, reading the Old Testament in Hebrew. Her lips would move slowly, methodically; her eyes would sparkle. She would tell me stories that stirred my imagination and made me dream of flying animals. My favorite was of a flying cow who laid an egg in space; from it an eagle hatched, rescuing the cow and bringing her down to earth. I never did figure out the moral of the story. Our grandmother was a pious, God-fearing woman who carefully kept track of the three of us. I remember her sharing her meals with the indigents who came knocking at our door, or taking care of a neighbor's sick children while their mother was away at the market. She was patient, charitable, and selfless.

When we moved into the cottage we brought along, among other things, a hardwood table that was placed in the middle of the veranda. This table served as the family gathering place. At it we ate and performed our chores. It also served as a dumping ground for most of our unwanted paraphernalia. In its drawer I kept my wooden soldiers, paper, and crayons. Between meals my grandmother used it for folding laundry, for sewing, and for general storage. If anybody was looking for anything, it could probably be found on or under the table, depending on the nature of the object. When no one was around, pigeons and other birds used the table as a meeting ground. This was the only time when my grandmother resented the presence of the table.

One morning soon after we were settled I heard Grandmother's high-pitched voice asking, "Where is the table? Did anyone see the table? It was here last night. . . ." We all got out of our beds, looked out, and saw that the veranda was empty. The table was gone. Who would bother to steal such a heavy table, we wondered. Mr. Joseph was as puzzled as we were and went off on horseback to notify the police some distance away. It was still early, and the morning dew covered the grass; the sun was rising slowly, and the fog was beginning to lift. One could see the moist air moving in waves above the fields and across the road, revealing the blue sky. We managed to have breakfast without the table, complaining to one another about the discomfort its absence caused us.

Soon a policeman arrived on bicycle, followed by Mr. Joseph on his puffing, sweating mare. The policeman talked briefly to my grandmother and immediately set to work. He found some footprints not far from our cottage, preserved in the still-moist ground. He cut a bit of straw, measured one

3

footprint with it, and painstakingly studied every inch of the impression. Every time he bent down his leather pouch would slide from his shoulder and get in his way. Slowly he would move it back into place, cursing under his breath.

The policeman was tall. He had graying hair and wore high, shiny black boots and a navy blue uniform with a tunic over it. Around the tunic he wore a wide leather belt; connected to it, crossing his chest, was a narrower one. Across his back he carried a rifle on a sling with a massive chamber and a highly polished stock. A large metal eagle, the emblem of the Polish Republic, was pinned to the center of his round navy blue cap.

That morning my brother's friend Tzytzek had come to visit, and before I realized it I found myself following the policeman with my brother, sister, and friend. He made no objection but asked us to be absolutely quiet. He dragged his bicycle along narrow paths through the barley and potato fields. Once in a while a pheasant or a hare would dart out from behind a bush, startling us. Whenever the policeman stopped to study a footprint he would put on his wire-rimmed glasses, which he cleaned regularly with a polka-dotted hand-kerchief. I wondered why he had to measure every footprint. Couldn't he identify them by sight? Tzytzek said in Yiddish, so the policeman wouldn't understand, that the cop wanted to show off because he had nothing better to do.

Soon the policeman got tired of dragging the dusty bicycle and asked Tzytzek to take it from him. As soon as Tzytzek took hold of the bicycle he tried out the bell, which scared off some birds nesting nearby. The policeman shouted at Tzytzek. I was afraid he might shoot him with his rifle if he tried to ring the bell again. It was getting hot, and the policeman started to perspire. He took off his tunic, trans-ferred the belts over his uniform, and, pointing at me, asked if I would like to carry the tunic for him. I agreed readily and put the rolled-up tunic under my right arm. It was heavy and cumbersome and smelled of disinfectant or some other chemi-cal that made me sneeze. Every time the policeman stopped to study a footprint I was tempted to put the tunic down, but I was afraid he might not like that. Tzytzek suggested I rest the tunic across the handlebars of the bicycle, but I proudly declined his offer and continued to carry it myself.

Before long we came to some railroad tracks, which the footprints crossed. On the other side we continued our search in the same manner: The policeman walked ahead, and we followed him, step by step, our eyes glued to him all the while. It was close to noon, and the sky was deep blue. Behind a cluster of trees we noticed a burned-out cottage with no roof; a thatch-roofed barn stood alongside. It was toward this place the policeman headed. There was not a soul in sight. A stray dog wandered by, sniffed the bicycle and Tzytzek's foot, and then disappeared. Tzytzek tried to kick him but missed. The policeman headed toward the barn, pushed open the door, and went inside. I heard a woman crying and begging for forgiveness. Soon the policeman reappeared leading a bare-foot, middle-aged couple. The woman kept crossing herself and crying; the man remained silent. He wore a pair of heavy, coarsely loomed pants and a collarless shirt full of holes. His hair was unkempt, his face covered with whiskers, and his forehead was punctuated by a wart the size of a cuff link. The woman was dressed just as shabbily; little bits of straw stuck to her hair and clothing. She didn't stop crossing herself for a moment.

The policeman ordered the couple to bring the table from the barn. They brought the top and the legs separately; they must have taken it apart so it would be easier to hide. The policeman decided that the man should carry the tabletop on his back, back to the farm, supporting it with heavy rope, and that we would help carry the legs. He took the bicycle back from Tzytzek and gave him a table leg in exchange. Tzytzek didn't like this one bit. He told us that if the couple could steal the table, they could carry it back as well. I also heard him tell my brother that in some countries they punished thieves by cutting off their hands so they couldn't steal again. Tzytzek thought this a good idea and said, "How else can you stop people from stealing?"

We started back with the policeman leading the procession, the man carrying the tabletop just behind him. His wife followed, still crying; we children brought up the rear. The policeman took back his tunic, enabling me to walk much faster. When we were about halfway home the policeman called a break and disappeared behind a big tree in the middle of a field. We could hear him urinating; in a loud voice he told us to take a rest. The man put the tabletop on the ground. He looked tired and scared and didn't say a word. He stared down at his bare feet and breathed heavily. After several minutes' rest we resumed our march. When we arrived at the cottage everyone came out to meet us; Grandmother had been worried about us, she said, even though Mr. Joseph had tried to reassure her, telling her that he saw us walking away with the policeman across the fields.

The policeman began questioning the couple, asking their names, their parents' names, their dates of birth, and their parents' dates of birth. He was trying to write a report of the case. They didn't know a thing or simply couldn't remember. The woman, through her tears, started to tell a story about how they had never in their lives owned a decent table. She admitted to the theft. Some weeks before, she added, a fire had almost destroyed their cottage with most of the things they owned, even the little clothing they had. My grandmother, hearing the woman's story, went inside the cottage and came back with a basket of fresh bread, farmer's cheese, and a jug of milk. She offered the food to the couple and urged them to eat. They must have been starved, for they devoured it. The policeman was surprised at my grandmother's feeding crooks, but he didn't interfere. Meanwhile, the table was reassembled and put back in place. The policeman turned impatiently to my grandmother and asked her if she wanted to press charges or to forget the whole episode. My grandmother said she felt that God had punished the couple enough with the fire and with their poverty. Why punish them more? The woman, upon hearing this, reached for my grandmother's hand, kissed it, and blessed her repeatedly. The policeman decided to drop the case but said he would take the thieves to the station for fingerprinting. Before they left my grandmother promised the woman that at the end of the summer she would receive the table as a gift. It was unbelievable. We thought she was fooling, but she really meant it.

The whole village talked of the table incident until we tired of hearing about it. The summer came to an end, we started packing, and on the very day we were to leave the couple showed up with a hand wagon. They had come for the table. In the wagon lay a large bouquet of freshly picked flowers; the man carried a live chicken under his arm. My grandmother was visibly moved by the gifts, and we all helped load the table on the wagon. The man handed the chicken to our grandmother; I could hear him say in his local Polish dialect, "God bless you, Mrs. Sarah, you are an angel." As the couple left my grandmother called out to them, "My name isn't Sarah, it's Elka, but it doesn't matter! It's only a name, and I forgive you for that, too." Then she turned back to the cottage, saying to herself, "Poor people."

I really hated to part with the table and my drawer, but now we had a live chicken to take home to Radom with us. On the way to the city in Mr. Joseph's wagon Grandmother sat next to me, caressing the chicken's head. Suddenly she looked up and asked, "How am I going to explain all this to your parents, can you tell me?" and she burst out laughing.

THE STUTTERER

I knew him most of my childhood. We were very good friends, as were our parents. He knew everything about me—even what I was thinking at a given time. I trusted and admired him despite his stutter. We went to the same school; I still remember my own dread when he was called to read aloud standing up. He stood there surrounded by his peers, silent, especially when faced with a word that began with a hard consonant like K. In the Polish language most words begin with consonants, but anything that started with the letter K was his special curse.

I even remember a particular word he struggled with: *kroki,* which means steps. Our reading teacher, a heavyset woman with very red cheeks and a lingering aroma of cheap perfume, stood in front of him, staring straight at him. He tried several times, but only a staccato sound like the rattling of a machine gun would come out of his mouth. His eyes closed, and tears rolled down his cheeks. He was told to sit down, and another boy was told to pick up the reading from there. To everyone's surprise, he, too, had a slight stutter; he could not complete an entire sentence. Though the teacher knew that those two boys

8

stuttered, she always asked them to read. She was a sadist, my friend said, taking pleasure in other people's suffering. I agreed, pleased to have learned a new word: sadist.

During recess I tried to comfort my friend. I never asked him questions about his stuttering. I took it that some people were born with it. I thought about other afflictions: blindness, retardation, being deaf-mute. I had once seen a legless man in a wheelchair being pushed by a lame young man, perhaps his son. I wondered which affliction would be most difficult or embarrassing to live with but couldn't make up my mind. I just felt very bad for my friend. I wanted to help but didn't know how.

I remembered reading in my brother's Greek history book the story about Demosthenes, a stutterer who was told by his teacher to fill his mouth with small pebbles and try to talk. According to the story, this is how Demosthenes cured his speech impediment. I told my friend this, but he thought it a fairy tale. The following day I took my brother's book to him, but he remained skeptical.

One year went by, and we entered the fifth grade. The readings were more difficult, and the same teacher—the sadist—was with us. She would call on my friend to read aloud; as before, he would stand silently looking at the page. Before long a number of boys started to stutter when reading. I suspected that they were mocking my friend. They did it in spite of themselves, however, and soon a good half of the class acquired a distinct speech impediment. It spread like an epidemic. The teacher wrote notes to their parents, warning them about their sons' final grades. There were early-morning conferences, a long exchange of parents' and teachers' letters, but still the stuttering went on.

My friend claimed that if he could sit down when reading he wouldn't be scared and perhaps wouldn't stutter. He insisted that standing made him self-conscious. I, too, developed a stutter and when reading aloud began to sound like my friend. I couldn't understand why I started to stutter; I never tried to imitate my friend, nor did I make fun of him. I became a subject of mockery and imitation for my fellow students, my relatives, and my two siblings. My uncle claimed that it was all psychological because I felt sorry for my friend; unable to help him, I became affected by his problem in some subconscious manner. I wasn't sure if I understood or agreed with him. I knew nothing about psychology, not even how to spell the word.

One day my father took me to a doctor who asked me if I was in a hurry when I urinated. I said no. "Well, then," he said, "since you can't rush urinating, why do you rush when you speak? You must slow down." I couldn't understand the connection, but I did try to speak slowly. It didn't help very much, so I suggested that my father write and ask the teacher to allow me to sit when called on to read. He did, but she refused. I practiced reading at home, standing up and sitting down, but the results were disappointing. The only time I didn't stutter was when I talked to myself. Since I couldn't talk to myself all the time, I kept quiet, read books, and stopped communicating with the adult world.

A year or so later World War II broke out. For practical reasons one had to know how to speak German. I found that the German language was more accommodating than Polish —it included fewer hard consonants, for starters—and soon I became fluent in it. Its similarity to Yiddish made me feel comfortable, and I stuttered less. I spoke as little Polish as I could get away with; I decided that the Polish language was hostile, and that it didn't like me.

I lost track of my friend during the war, but I thought often of him, of the reading sessions, and of our frustrations. Thirty-five years later, while visiting Israel, I found out that he lived in Tel Aviv. When I called I controlled my breathing and spoke slowly. I managed to tell him clearly, in Polish, who I was. A strange feeling of anxiety about my own stutter overtook me. I didn't want him to think that I remembered his stutter or that I was trying to make fun of him.

There was silence, and then, in an evenly measured, resonant voice, my friend informed me that he was packing for a

THE STUTTERER

European lecture tour, but that he planned to be in New York
before long, where we might be able to see each other. He was
scheduled to teach on mental disorders and speech impedi-
ments at a medical school. He was a professor of psychiatry. I
was tempted to ask him if he still read standing up but didn't
think it would be appropriate. He managed to inquire whether
I still stuttered.

THE WEDDING
PICTURE

I vividly remember the picture of Uncle Hershel and his bride Annette. It was the size of a postcard, or perhaps a bit larger, and it was sepia-toned. My mother displayed it with other family heirlooms and artifacts in a leaded glass cabinet, part of a massive, walnut-stained breakfront in our dining room. There was a musical clock that didn't tell time, but the music box worked. I can still remember the tune. The clock and the picture were central to our household's mysteries.

Whenever I studied the wedding picture I also liked to listen to the musical clock. Its melody reminded me of a wedding march, lively and cheerful. Uncle Hershel looked as though he was in his thirties—suave, serious, imposing. His bride, Annette, a brunette with a becoming hairdo and a sweet, soft smile, looked friendly; I had the feeling she was looking straight at me, while Uncle Hershel focused on something far away. I imagined her as someone who liked children.

I was told that they lived in Paris, France, which to me, at the age of nine, seemed the other end of the world. My mother, who was Uncle Hershel's older sister, kept reassuring me that one day we would all go to Paris, perhaps for good. I thought it was a good idea, and secretly I hoped that we would move soon. Most of my mother's relatives were living abroad, except for her younger sister Dora, who was about to leave for Palestine. Aunt Dora was young and pretty and never forgot to bring me candy when she came to visit. I felt sorry for my mother after Aunt Dora left; soon my grandmother followed, and all her close relatives were gone. My father's relatives were around, including his parents, but he wasn't—for some reason no one had explained to me—on speaking terms with them.

The wedding picture became my link to the outside world. I could picture Paris from the postcards that we received periodically from Uncle Hershel. Two were displayed on either side of the wedding picture: One was of the Eiffel Tower and the other of the Arc de Triomphe. To me, those two landmarks were wonders of the world. When my friends came to visit I would wind the clock and show off the postcards and the wedding picture. Then I would give them a short lecture about the Paris landmarks and about my Uncle Hershel and his bride as though I was an expert.

I really didn't know much about my Uncle Hershel, but the picture suggested that he must be very important, if not very rich. I never read his letters, since they were written in Yiddish and I wasn't able to decipher his handwriting. This gave fuel to my fantasies. I would carry on imaginary conversations with the picture, ask questions; at times Hershel and Annette spoke to me. The wedding picture became my icon.

Sometime in the thirties, shortly after she left for Palestine, Aunt Dora included a picture in one of her letters. She was photographed with the man she was about to marry. The picture was smaller than Uncle Hershel's. In the cabinet it was obscured by the seams in the leaded glass. Aunt Dora didn't smile in the picture; she appeared very buxom, and her fiancé partially bald. When, as a child, I had visited her, I had occasionally had to sleep in her bed. She would put her arms around me, enveloping me in the abundance of her breasts. How I hated to get up in the morning and put my feet on the cold floor! The mere thought that she would sleep with her new husband made me dislike him.

A few years went by. The war broke out, we were under Nazi occupation, and no more mail came in. One day we had to give up our apartment and move to a newly created ghetto in another part of the city. We had to leave most of our furniture behind, including the massive breakfront. In the haste of packing and looking for another place to live we left the pictures and the musical clock. I managed to remember the wedding picture, however. When the ghetto was liquidated and I was sent to the camps, in the saddest moments of my incarceration I remembered Uncle Hershel's wedding picture and Annette's warm smile.

Shortly after the end of the war I managed to get to Paris. Uncle Hershel didn't know I was coming, but I had memorized his address, along with the addresses of my other relatives, and as soon as I arrived I went and knocked at his door. A husky, middle-aged man, unshaven, wearing a pair of soiled slacks and a torn sweatshirt, greeted me. Before I had a chance to introduce myself he spoke.

"We must be related. You look just like my sister. Are you by any chance my nephew?"

"Yes, Uncle Hershel, I'm your nephew," I answered.

He was visibly shaken. His eyes filled with tears, and we embraced; I could tell that he knew my parents were dead. A sadness emanated from him, though he tried to smile. The little apartment wasn't very tidy. It looked as though it had not been cleaned in months and smelled quite stale. There was no trace of a woman's presence.

I remembered the stories my mother used to tell her friends about Uncle Hershel's beautiful place and the swanky *arrondissement* where he lived. The small apartment was a third-floor walk-up in an old, neglected building with large patches of plaster missing. The neighborhood was not at all beautiful. It sat right in the middle of a working-class quarter teeming with panhandlers, street vendors, and prostitutes. It reverberated with loud noises; different languages could be heard everywhere.

I was tempted to ask Uncle Hershel about Annette, but I didn't have the courage. What if something awful had happened to her during the war? I kept hoping that he himself would tell me. He sat across from me, recounting what a terrible war it had been and how concerned he had been about all of us, how difficult it had been for him, too. According to his story, he had fought with the French underground against the Nazis. One day he had gotten very sick and had to be hidden at a farm until the war was over. It was risky to find medical help, but somehow he had survived. He considered it a miracle he was alive.

Suddenly I realized that this stranger and I had very little in common other than the fact that he was my mother's brother. He didn't even resemble the uncle I knew in the picture. It offended my memory. How could I accept this stranger without the beautiful, smiling face of the woman next to him? When our conversation came to a long pause I asked him on impulse, "How is Aunt Annette, and where is she?" At first he looked at me, puzzled; then, focusing his eyes on something far away, just as in the wedding picture, he told me, "Annette and I were divorced some years ago. We couldn't get along. I didn't want to write about it to your mother—I wanted to save her the embarrassment and the worry."

I was shocked and dismayed. "Does this mean that I'll never meet her?" I asked him.

"No, not at all," he answered. "I think that can be arranged. We're friends, and we see each other from time to time. But why do you want to meet her?" he asked. I, not having a better reason, told him of my long romance with their wedding picture, how I liked Annette's smile, and how happy I was to know that she was my aunt.

Uncle Hershel looked at me in disbelief. I could tell by his astonished expression that he felt as if he were witnessing a resurrection. I had to add that he, too, looked handsome and elegant in that picture, even though he wasn't smiling. His expression hardly changed—just a faint lifting of one corner of his mouth.

Two days later Uncle Hershel called me at my other uncle's house, where I was staying. He asked me to meet him that evening at his house; the three of us were to go out for supper. I was very excited and thought all day long of the meeting. Since he and Annette were divorced, he asked me not to call her "aunt."

On the appointed evening I joined Uncle Hershel, and together we took the Métro to meet Annette. He appreciated my punctuality and told me so. My uncle was still a very handsome man: tall, erect, graying at the temples. He wore a double-breasted dark suit and a very colorful silk tie. Annette was waiting for us when we arrived. I was introduced to her; we shook hands, and she uttered only one word, *"Enchantée."* We decided to walk to the restaurant; in all the time it took us to get there she asked me just one question: "How do you like Paris?" I replied, "I like it a lot."

Annette was hardly the same person I remembered from the wedding picture. Her hair was different, she was turning gray, and her face was beginning to show wrinkles. She was a bit heavy, but her hands were amazingly thin, with long fingers. She wore a gray summer suit with a silk scarf around her neck, which gave her some color. She didn't wear any makeup, but I could detect a pleasant scent of perfume. I decided that the two of them were tasteful dressers, and somehow this pleased me.

Uncle Hershel took us to a restaurant with Jewish cooking. It was a bit crowded when we arrived, but soon we were seated in a quiet corner. I was facing Annette; Uncle Hershel sat to my left. It was his favorite table, he told me. Annette looked at me with a faint smile and asked me point-blank, "Why did you want to meet me, if you don't mind telling me?"

I didn't know where to begin; I had hardly expected her to ask me such a question. Fifteen different thoughts came to my mind. I must have turned red; Annette, noticing it, smiled and turned to Uncle Hershel. "Your uncle tells me how you still remember us from the wedding picture. Is that right? Can you still recognize us? Are we the same people? Do you think I'm the same person? Tell me and be frank."

"Yes," I said, "when you smile you're the same." My voice quavered, and I felt embarrassed. I didn't want to offend her, and I wasn't sure that I hadn't. I realized I had nothing to say. I was just a kid who had been infatuated with a woman's smile and now, eleven years later, faced with reality, was trying to back out. I felt bad. Reality didn't live up to my memory.

I started to feel sorry for them. Why had they divorced? Without giving it another thought, I asked, "What is the point of being divorced? Isn't it lonely without a companion all these years?" They were stunned. Naturally they hadn't expected this young man before them to preach on the immorality of being divorced, let alone pass judgment on their private lives. "Forgive me," I said, "I know it's none of my business, but seeing you together, I couldn't help it, since you're my relatives, and I feel as if I have known you most of my life."

Annette laughed. I could tell that she didn't mind what I had said. "You talk like an experienced man, and you aren't even married. I assume you don't know what it is to have a bad marriage. In the beginning your uncle and I were happy. We had a good marriage, except that we didn't know how to appreciate it. I must admit that there was too much interference on the part of some of my relatives. In this respect, your uncle had a case." Uncle Hershel sat there sipping his drink, quiet, contemplative, his eyes focused on something far away.

It was late in the evening, and the restaurant was almost empty; it was time for us to leave. We started back, escorting Annette to her place. She lived with her old invalid father. She was in a very good mood, and I had a feeling that she liked me. On the way the two of them pointed out several Paris landmarks; as we crossed the Champs Elysées I saw the Arc de Triomphe and, further in the distance, the Eiffel Tower.

There was a festive mood in the air. Paris was getting ready to celebrate Bastille Day, Annette told me. I had only two more days before going back to Germany, my temporary home, where I worked for the U.S. Army. We walked for a long time, and I listened to their recollections of the good old days, of the time before the war.

We were all exhausted by the time the evening ended. As I kissed Annette good-bye it dawned on me that she hadn't changed as drastically as I had first thought. I told her how much I had enjoyed meeting her; if she didn't have any objections, I asked, might I call her "aunt"? "I would love it very much if you did," she answered. Her soft, warm smile was indeed still there.

The following day I went to say good-bye to Uncle Hershel. In his apartment I noticed a copy of the wedding picture sitting on top of a dresser inside an old dusty frame. I stood transfixed and speechless. This was what I really wanted, the picture. Could my uncle get me a copy of it? I inquired. "I don't see why not," he said. "I promise to order one and mail it to you."

Soon I emigrated to America. Some years went by, but the picture never arrived, and I was too embarrassed to remind my uncle about it. A few years later, in the early 1950s, I received a letter from Uncle Hershel announcing that he and Annette had remarried; inside the envelope I found a new wedding picture. This time the picture was a bit smaller, but it was sepia-toned like the first one. The two of them looked a little older; Uncle Hershel still had his faraway look, but Annette's smile was almost identical to the way I had remembered it from years before.

THE VIOLIN

Many years ago, before I turned seven, I found an old violin on one of my weekend visits to my grandfather's attic. It sat in a beautifully constructed wooden case lined with velvet that must once have been green but was by then so faded it was almost colorless. Next to it, held by two wooden clips, was the bow. Some of its hair was torn, and it hung loosely, partially covering the neck of the violin.

"This violin was made by Giuseppe Guarneri," my grandfather told me, "the best Italian violin maker of the eighteenth century. There's even a label inside the violin attesting to it. Not only is the violin old and rare, it's also very valuable," he assured me. Lowering his voice, he added, "Whoever in the family takes violin lessons will one day get to keep the Guarneri."

I was very tempted. Grandfather even let me touch one of the instrument's strings, the only one still in place. The other three were broken. It gave out a sad, prolonged sound, as if it were calling for help.

"Of course, the violin is in bad shape, and it needs to be repaired," Grandfather said. "One day I'll take it to Warsaw to one of the best repairmen I know. He'll take care of it properly."

The violin remained on my mind for days after; sometimes in my dreams I could hear the sound of the lonely string. My older sister had been studying the violin for some weeks and didn't like it a bit. She complained often about the pain in her wrists and the stiff neck she got from holding the violin under her chin. Eventually she quit her lessons. At that time my father decided I would be next to take violin lessons. With my grandfather's promise in mind I readily agreed. I started my lessons on a half-size instrument and, to my dismay, discovered that I would not require a full-size violin like the Guarneri in my grandfather's attic until I was in my teens and my arms were much longer.

My lessons continued for years; on my visits with my grandfather I inquired always about repairing the Guarneri, assuring him that very soon I would be ready for a full-size instrument. It was my sixth year of studying the violin. Sometimes I would bring along my own violin to show him how unacceptably small it was. He kept putting me off, promising the Guarneri to me later.

In 1938, one year before World War II broke out, my grandfather died, and some of the things in his attic— including the violin—were given to me. Now that the violin was in my possession I examined it and read its label over and over again. I was fourteen, and mesmerized by the Guarneri. I decided to try to repair it myself. I was able to replace the broken strings, I installed a new bridge, and I even rubbed in some shellac to restore the long-lost shine. When I finally tried the gleaming instrument I discovered it had the richest, sweetest tone I had ever heard. I was enthralled by the sound; I only felt sorry that my grandfather couldn't be there to hear me play.

We were living under Nazi occupation, and soon various decrees came out calling for the confiscation of privately

owned musical instruments, radios, and even fur coats. I
could not have turned in the Guarneri to the Nazis. My father
felt the same way about the family fur coats as I did about the
violin, and, together with my uncle and a trusted Polish
friend, Mr. Bolek, we filled a metal trunk with furs, added the
Guarneri, and managed to bury it in the yard behind the row
of wooden coal bins. On a moonless night the trunk was
lowered into a hole in the ground lined with several layers of
thick tar paper. It was past curfew, and the yard was deserted,
except for an occasional stray cat looking for a place to spend
the night. I acted as the lookout, monitoring every suspicious
sound. It was a cold, dark night, and the sound of the dirt
hitting the trunk reminded me of my grandfather's funeral.
Chills crept up my spine.

The following day I spoke to Mr. Bolek about the violin and
tried to impress upon him how much it meant to me. He just
listened and, putting his hand on my shoulder, assured me,
"One day you'll play this violin again, I can tell." Soon I had
to turn in my own suddenly precious violin to the Nazi
authorities; with no instrument left I had a stronger urge to
practice than ever before. I memorized most of my music and
kept practicing by humming.

During my time in Nazi camps I lost awareness of ever
having played the violin and very rarely thought of the
Guarneri. The thing that stayed in my mind was the sad sound
of the lonely string. At times I would imagine hearing a violin
somewhere in my past, a long time before. Not until after the
war was over did I have a chance to listen to someone else play
a real violin. It filled me with nostalgia and made me think of
my long-lost Guarneri.

Two years after the war's end I emigrated to America.
Immediately I wrote a letter to Mr. Bolek. Some months later
it came back marked "addressee unknown." I feared that
something must have happened to him and wrote a second
letter to the Polish Red Cross. Still no luck; they couldn't

locate him. It wasn't until the late 1960s that I managed—by a small miracle—to contact our old friend. He informed me that after the war he had been transferred to another area in Poland, and for the longest time he kept inquiring about us through the International Red Cross, also to no avail. Now that he had retired from his work he was back in our home town, Radom; he assured me that the contents of our trunk were safe in his possession.

I gave him permission to make use of the furs but asked him to arrange, if possible, the shipment of the violin to America. Mr. Bolek informed me that since the violin was old and very valuable, the Polish authorities would not allow it to leave the country. It had been classified as an antiquity, and we would need a permit from the Ministry of Culture, which refused to issue one. He tried everything possible, but nothing worked. I had nothing to prove that I was the rightful owner of the violin; there were no papers or bill of sale. This bothered me no end; my Guarneri remained a prisoner in Poland.

In America I bought a used violin and started practicing for my own enjoyment. It wasn't the same; I had lost the skill I had had twenty-five years earlier, and the instrument sounded flat. I found that my coordination was off, and that my left arm went numb. I thought of taking a refresher course, but since I considered myself somewhat advanced, and since I was past forty, I was embarrassed to have to start from the beginning. If I only had the Guarneri, I kept telling myself, my skills would certainly improve. Perhaps the frustration over losing it had made me forget how to play, I theorized; soon I decided to give up the violin for good. The Guarneri, of course, remained always in the back of my mind; I thought one day the mailman would simply deliver it.

In the summer of 1983 I was assigned by the magazine I worked for to do a photographic assignment in Poland. I visited Radom and managed to track down Mr. Bolek. He was old and not well, and his eyesight was failing. He could hardly recognize me, but he had no trouble remembering our link, the buried Guarneri. When he saw me he put his arm around me; in a sad voice he told me how sorry he was to hear about my parents, and how happy he was to know that the three children had survived.

Mr. Bolek's apartment was small and full of old furniture. The walls were covered with old photographs, paintings, and mementos from a century ago. Next to his chair stood a small table covered with an assortment of medicine bottles and a saucer full of eyedroppers.

"It's so nice to see you as an adult," Mr. Bolek said. "I remember you when you were a little boy. I used to see you with your violin case under your arm going to your music lesson. Your school was right around the corner from where I used to live. That was on Focha Street. But the school is gone now, like so many other things."

Mr. Bolek paused for a few seconds. "For many years your father and I were good friends," he said. "We never had any quarrels and always respected each other. Now it's a different world; people are different from the way we used to be. But what can you do? Now let me show you something."

He walked over to his wardrobe and withdrew my violin case. He put it on the table and ceremoniously proceeded to open it. The violin was guarded by a lock and key, which I was certain it had not been before. Mr. Bolek took out the violin, wrapped in a sheet of green felt. Slowly, painstakingly, he removed the instrument from the fabric. I was in awe. The violin gleamed like a highly polished jewel. Everything was in place; I could hardly tell this was the same instrument. Holding the violin, Mr. Bolek turned to me and in a shaky voice told me, "All these years I had a feeling that one day you would come back to get the violin. Some years ago, after I retired, I decided to learn how to fix violins, with the idea of repairing your Guarneri. Before I knew, I got so involved I started repairing other people's violins, until my eyesight deteriorated and I had to give it up."

When he finished speaking he pulled a handkerchief from

his pocket and started wiping his eyes. I thought he was crying. "I don't know how I'll ever be able to repay you for saving and repairing the violin for me," I blurted out, moved.

"You don't owe me anything, my friend," he answered. "I should be the one to thank you. Since the day I first set eyes on this violin it has changed my life. It gave me a sense of responsibility, it made me love music, and it motivated me to become a repairman. It was given to me in trust, and it became an important link in our friendship. It was almost like taking care of a friend. I also knew how much it had meant to you, the musician. You see, it worked for me in so many ways. Now you have to find a way to get it to America.

"Here, it's yours," he said, grinning proudly as he handed over the Guarneri to me. I held it by the neck and saw my own beaming reflection in the polished top of the instrument. I touched the strings; the violin let out a clear, off-key, vibrant sound. I took the bow and started tuning it, though I wasn't sure I still remembered how. I was speechless; my hands shook. When I thought I had the violin tuned I gently returned it to its case. I was moved by this gesture of friendship and took Mr. Bolek's hand, shaking it vigorously, until I noticed a pained expression on his lined face.

There was no way to get permission from the Ministry of Culture to export the violin, I was informed; the laws remained in place. I decided to risk carrying my prize out of the country with me. I had visions of being arrested for smuggling antiquities out of Poland and ending up, after so many years, in a Polish jail. But the following day I was on the plane with the violin at my side, on my way home. No one had asked any questions; it was as if they hadn't noticed the battered case I carried. I was elated. After forty-two years the Guarneri was free again.

Almost one year after I left Poland with my Guarneri I received a letter from Mr. Bolek, written by his daughter, Lucyna. He inquired whether I was happy with the Guarneri and told me he hoped the violin was being well taken care of. He had bought an old violin for himself so that he wouldn't

THE VIOLIN

feel a complete loss. "Strange," wrote his daughter, "how one could get attached to an instrument as if it were a person." Her father kept the old violin in his wardrobe, in the same spot where he had kept the Guarneri, and even though he couldn't see anymore he could still hold it and tune it (though not very well); sometimes he tried to play some of the songs he had played on the Guarneri. Occasionally he would complain to her about the flat tones the violin produced; it didn't compare to the Guarneri, he would comment. Still, it gave him a great deal of pleasure, his daughter wrote.

MASHA

For years I would hear her shuffle down the length of the corridor to the door of our apartment in her deceased husband's oversized boots. She would set the two large canisters of milk down on the cement floor and gently knock. She was middle-aged, of massive build, with a broad, prematurely wrinkled face and large, wide-set gray eyes. There was a kind look about her. In the winter she would wrap a heavy woolen shawl over her head and shoulders and tie the ends behind her back. On her hands she wore gloves with the fingertips cut off so that she could handle her measuring cup. When she entered the apartment puffs of steam rose from her nostrils; one could see tiny icicles sticking to her eyebrows. She was our milk woman.

Usually my grandmother, who handled the milk transactions, asked the woman to stay for a minute and warm up, but she politely declined. There were other people waiting for milk, she would say. But one day she promised to drop in for a chat after she had completed her rounds. Some time later she did come to see us and, in fact, stayed most of the afternoon. She spoke to my grandmother about her difficult life and said she needed some advice. She was concerned about her teenage daughter Masha, who, due to an accident, had become a deaf-mute.

Evidently Masha was born a healthy, normal child. She was a happy little girl and was loved by her parents and her two siblings. Her father was a cobbler, and the family had managed to survive the difficult times of the Depression, but he had died when Masha was six, and their lives had not been the same since. The milk woman had become the sole supporter of the family, and her other two children, already in their late teens, left home for a kibbutz in Palestine. She had been left alone with Masha. When she went on her milk rounds she would leave Masha with trusted neighbors who had children of their own; Masha was safe and liked to stay with them. They had a girl Masha's age, and the two of them liked to play together. And this was how Masha had been finding her own way, mostly alone and away from her mother.

One day when the milk woman had come back for Masha she found her hiding in a corner in tears with her dress torn and her face scratched. According to Masha's playmate, the neighbor's nephew, a retarded teenager, had come to visit, and while his aunt was out on an errand he had attacked Masha and nearly—or actually—raped her. Masha had gone into shock and lost the powers of speech and hearing. Her mother took her to a doctor, to a rabbi, even to a witch doctor. The doctor told her that Masha was still in a state of shock, and that one day soon she would speak again. The rabbi told her to keep giving *tzedaka,* to be patient, that the Almighty would help. The witch doctor put some hot coals into a pot of water and used the steam to anoint Masha on the forehead and behind her ears.

Years went by and nothing happened; Masha remained silent. The milk woman was desperate and didn't know to whom to turn for help. In the everyday drudgery of her milk rounds she was hoping to find salvation for Masha. She also thought that Masha understood her limitations, and that she would have to come to terms with the sad reality of growing up a deaf-mute. The doctor didn't know enough about it and couldn't tell if Masha was even conscious of the fact that she had once been able to talk. If she knew as much, she wasn't giving any indications of it. The milk woman herself wasn't well and some days had to stay home in bed and rest, while Masha, withdrawn and frightened, sat opposite her for hours, staring. If something happened to her, who would take care of Masha? She refused to think of institutions, even if there was one that would take her daughter. She was determined never to give Masha up, no matter what.

My grandmother asked the milk woman to bring Masha the next time she came around; she would like to meet her.

Not long after, one Sunday morning we were in the kitchen finishing breakfast when Masha walked in with her mother. She was a stunning child. She had a full oval face with high cheekbones and almond-shaped blue eyes with long lashes. Her thick flaxen hair was smoothly combed into two braids that hung over her shoulders. The roundness of her ample breasts was accentuated by the tightness of her frayed dress. There was something sensuous and voluptuous about her that could even attract the attention of a child; I was only twelve years old and still innocent of any erotic desires, but Masha stirred something in me, even if I didn't know what it was.

She carried a small wicker basket with a doll in it. Even at her age—she must have been about my age—she still played with the doll and treated it as if it was her baby. She even took it to bed with her, we were told.

My mother smiled at Masha and took her hand. Masha's face lit up, and she leaned her head against my mother. I was jealous and felt betrayed, and I walked out into the courtyard. I tried to understand what was happening; I was afraid that if Mother showed affection to another child—an outsider at that—she couldn't love her own child, too. To me it was a matter of mathematics. If you have ten apples and you give away some, you don't have ten apples anymore. It bothered me even though I knew that Masha had her own mother and that she would leave soon. Still, I stayed in the yard bouncing a ball until Masha and her mother appeared. When Masha noticed me she waved, and a long sound came out of her throat. It disturbed me, as I didn't know what she meant. Still, I was mesmerized by her and waved back at her.

My mother claimed that Masha needed love and affection, especially after the dreadful accident that had nearly destroyed her. I still didn't know what incident she was referring to; when I inquired I was told that Masha had fallen out of a window. The milk woman, my mother told me, didn't have the time to go about demonstrating love. Life was difficult for her, and most of her time was spent in overcoming obstacles. She cared about Masha; after all, Masha was her own flesh and blood. She worked hard to support her, provided her with food and clothing, but that was all she could do for her daughter. My mother spoke about affection as if it were a medicine; my grandmother was of the opinion that Masha most probably blamed her mother for the accident. Whenever I happened to be around during the discussions—which was often, as Masha's plight was a constant topic of conversation in our household—it was not a rape Masha had suffered, but an accident. I heard endless analyses and discussions of its psychological ramifications.

The whole story about the window accident sat poorly with me. I became suspicious when I came into the kitchen unexpectedly one night and my grandmother quickly changed the subject. I had heard her mention Masha's name, but as soon as she noticed me she started talking about her forthcoming trip to Palestine to live with my aunts, and how she wanted to be buried there when she died. She referred to Palestine as her home and the land of Abraham, Jacob, and Sarah.

Shortly after my grandmother left for Palestine my parents moved to a small town not far from Radom and started a business there. We lost track of the milk woman and Masha, but my mother continued to discuss Masha and her predicament with a lady she befriended in the new community. I was commuting to my old school by train and hardly ever thought about Masha or her mother. If I hadn't dreamt about Masha one night I would probably never have thought of her again. In my dream she appeared naked, crying and carrying a bouquet of roses. She handed me the roses; I tried to reach for them and pricked my fingers on the thorns. I woke up screaming with pain; I could feel the pain in my fingers for days after.

The dream preoccupied me, so much so that I told a friend about it. He thought for a while and decided that I should either have my head examined or write a letter to Dr. Sigmund Freud. Instead I went to see my Uncle Joseph, who owned a considerable number of books on erotica and was well versed in the subject. I was especially fascinated with one of his books, titled *Die Geschichte Of Die Erotische Kunst.* I also found a book in his house that dealt with the interpretation of dreams. The books were in German, a language I didn't yet know, and contained the most elaborate illustrations. I couldn't find anything that referred to a female in the nude carrying a bouquet of roses. My uncle was broad-minded enough to offer his own interpretation when I told him about my dream, however: He stated matter-of-factly that I could consider myself a man.

I forgot about the dream before long, but not about Masha, who often came back to disturb my sleep. This went on for nearly two years. In the meantime we had moved back to the city, and I had graduated from public school. I was now fifteen years old, preparing for exams to enter middle school.

Early in the summer of 1939, some months before war broke out, I went with my friend to visit his grandparents, who lived on the outskirts of our city. It was a long walk, and we had to cross a field. As we were nearing the edge of the field I saw, to my amazement, Masha sitting on a tree stump, reading. I wasn't going to stop, but when she looked up and saw me her face lit up, and a long sound poured out of her throat; it was inarticulate, but it was unmistakably her name. She looked as stunning as before, only more mature. She kept bowing and touching her heart; I stared at her and blushed. She went over to her basket and took out a piece of paper;

using the tree stump as a table, she wrote a message for me. "I can read and write now, and I know sign language," it said. Her handwriting was very childish, and the line included several misspellings, but clearly Masha could now express herself. She looked straight into my eyes; my whole face burned. I managed only to take the paper from her and write, "Please come to see us any time," along with our address. Then I walked away with my friend, waving good-bye until I lost sight of her.

After that encounter I became obsessed with Masha. Hardly a minute went by when I wasn't thinking of her or imagining her in the most unusual settings. I still wasn't sure why, but I certainly liked being near her. She never did come to see us again, and soon it was September; the war broke out, and everything changed drastically.

At one point my mother found out that the milk woman had died and that Masha had gone to work for a well-to-do couple as a maid. This was the last time I heard her name mentioned in our household; eventually her image began to dissolve.

In the summer of 1942 the Nazis decided to deport most of the Jews from our city. The night before the deportation I went into hiding with my brother, as our mother had begged us to do. The following day I was betrayed and escorted back to the ghetto under SS armed escort. At night, when it was over, I was left behind with several hundred others, some of whom were selected to clean the ghetto of its dead and their belongings.

We were taken to a dark side street where we saw corpses everywhere: on sidewalks, in doorways, in courtyards. People of all ages were strewn about in the most grotesque positions, some still clutching their belongings, others with their knapsacks attached to their backs. Pools of blood were visible wherever there was a hollow in the unevenly paved sidewalk. As daylight broke we were able to distinguish more horror: piles of clothing, bundles of personal items, some food. Liquids and jams flowed out of broken jars into the gutters, where they mixed with blood. Books and torn documents, baby shoes and broken eyeglasses lay scattered in the middle of the street. The SS men guarding us were merciless. With fixed bayonets they urged us on, screaming, cursing, and bringing their rifle butts down on our backs as we cleared.

We worked as fast as was humanly possible. I could feel the early-morning chill, and still I was hot. Streams of sweat ran down my back. I was shaken by the gruesome sight of so many dead children, some with horrified expressions still on their faces. I got gooseflesh; it felt like an electric current was hitting my skin.

"Murderers, savages, you shall burn in Hell one day," I kept repeating to myself, disbelieving what my eyes showed me.

At one point I stopped to pick up a dead body and nearly fainted as I reached for the legs. It was Masha. I thought my heart would stop. We worked in teams of two; I was hardly able to follow the footsteps of my partner, who took hold of Masha's arms. I followed, holding on to her legs. In my sorrow I tried to recite the prayer for the dead. *"Yisgadal Veyiska-dash,"* I muttered under my breath, entirely unable to remember the rest of the prayer.

"Where art Thou, O God? Look what is happening to Your children." That was all I could think of, and that is what I remember today. I didn't think I could make it to the end of the street. My legs were buckling under, and I was near collapse. When finally we lay the body down on top of a pile of others I noticed a cloth tag sewn to her dress. In large, hand-printed letters it spelled: MASHA A DEAF-MUTE.

MR. G.

As far back as I can remember I would see Mr. Gutman in our house in Radom. He was a diminutive man with a pear-shaped head covered by a tightly fitting, worn-out cap in which he stashed shipping orders. There were always at least three copies, tissue-thin, wrinkled, and greasy from his balding pate. A cigarette butt protruded from his lips; inevitably one wondered how long he could hold on to it before getting burned. His long, neglected mustache was discolored from nicotine; the true color of his remaining hair was indeterminable. Dressed in a coat of heavy, dark gray fabric with patches that didn't exactly match, he appeared always with an old, bulging leather pouch slung across his chest, which only added to his awkward shape.

Though he was very thin and sickly-looking, Mr. Gutman's exuberance and animation were unflagging. One day my father told me that Mr. G.—as he called him—was a very important person. An expediter, his job was to insure that local merchants expecting goods by rail or truck received them on time and in good order. He was a frequent guest in our store, and in our house when the store was closed. He loved to debate with my father over a glass of tea, mainly about politics, anti-Semitism in Poland, or the rise of Nazism in Germany. He was somewhat prescient, for I remember him urging my father to pack up the family and emigrate. The debates lasted into the evening with my mother replenishing the tea.

Sometimes I was allowed to sit and listen, and after a number of sessions I grew very fond of Mr. G. He had few teeth left but insisted on biting into hard lumps of sugar. Every time he took a bite I was sure he would crack a remaining tooth; he showed no signs of distress.

My mother would ask him to take off his pouch and coat and relax, but he would decline apologetically. He didn't feel right without it, he would say; after all, the pouch was part of him. There was something theatrical and sad about Mr. G. He once told us about his family—an asthmatic wife who dreamt of an apartment with big windows, and a son who wanted to be a lawyer. Being Jewish and poor didn't guarantee very much, he said. He spoke always with conviction, never questioning anything. His word was final. His debates were endless, full of slogans, proverbs, and biblical analogies. He never remembered my name and always referred to me by my brother's name, Michael. My mother would correct him, but he would forget almost immediately. To him I was Michael. I did not dare contradict him over anything, not even my own name.

One Chanukah evening during a snowstorm Mr. G. showed up with some papers for my father to sign. His cap and pouch were covered with a heavy layer of snow. After depositing his oversized rubber boots in the hallway he came into the kitchen and with one fast motion of his right hand managed to flick the snow off his pouch into the sink; he then slowly leaned over the sink and did the same to his cap. I was impressed. That evening was the first time that Mr. G. took off his pouch and parked it on the floor next to his chair. My mother urged him to join us for potato *latkes* and tea. He slipped into the corner chair so as not to take up too much room, talking as he ate. Tiny particles of food flew out of his mouth as he spoke. My father was the butt of the spray and did his best to dodge it. I sat next to the kitchen stove, watching and enjoying every minute of it.

Suddenly Mr. G. turned toward me and, squinting his tiny blue eyes, asked if I could tell him the significance of Chanukah. I began to recite all I knew, but he turned to my father, saying, "What do you do with kids who know all the answers? You've got to watch them, they're dangerous." After a pause he added, "What can you teach a smart kid, huh?"

Occasionally I would see him rush by me in the street, frail, stooped over, affixed to his eternal leather pouch. I would try to greet him, but he ran too fast to hear or notice me. These were the thirties, and times were hard: Depression, unemployment, and not much to look forward to. The Depression was a favorite topic for Mr. G. Some of the hard-luck stories he told were very sad. He always managed to know a widow with small children who couldn't pay the coalman or the baker, a well-to-do son who refused to help his destitute parents, or some case ending in suicide. He knew how to tell a story.

He wasn't religious or God-fearing. He swore God was on a prolonged vacation or in exile. I listened attentively and believed every word he uttered. Then came the Spanish Civil War, and Mr. G. was consumed by it. He blamed the whole world for letting the fascists destroy Spain, saw the imminent rise of Nazism everywhere. His pessimism rubbed off on all of us, and we began to think as he did. I was only twelve years old, but thanks to Mr. G. I was getting a firm grasp of world events. Eventually I carried my knowledge to my classroom, only to find that it wasn't exactly welcome. My history teacher failed to see eye to eye with Mr. G. He announced that anyone who disagreed with Generalissimo Francisco Franco was a communist. The next time I saw Mr. G. at our house I relayed this piece of information to him, and he nearly collapsed. I had never seen him so upset. He started a harangue about reactionaries and fascism of such intensity that I was left dumbfounded. I hardly understood what he was saying; still, I listened. Finally, after a long and exhaustive lecture, he concluded that my teacher was insane, but I shouldn't tell him so; it would be our secret.

Shortly after this incident I read a story in my father's newspaper about the bombing of a town in Spain called Guernica; the picture showed piles of rubble with human corpses everywhere. This was the first time I had seen anything like that in print. In my mind I connected the Guernica story with everything Mr. G. related during his evening sessions: the evils of war, the Polish senate with Endek Senators and their reactionary stooges, the rise of Nazism, and the burning of the Reichstag. I began to clip news items about the Spanish Civil War, the Depression, and other world calamities. Soon I had a drawerful of very dramatic clips; I didn't know what to do with them, but I kept them nevertheless. Every time I looked at a Guernica picture I imagined Mr. G. standing behind it with clenched fists, screaming at the world to stop.

One day during Passover Mr. G. showed up without his leather pouch. He was dressed in a heavyweight navy blue suit and an olive-green spring coat with a dark green velvet collar. He even wore a slightly wrinkled tie. Everything he wore was unfamiliar to us except his cap—he just couldn't part with that, it seemed. He came in as we were settling down for a feast of Passover pancakes; my mother invited him to join us. He was seated next to me. I soon became very uncomfortable from the strong smell of nicotine emanating from him. He kept puffing away, and clouds of smoke soon hung over the entire table. No one in our family smoked, and everyone started coughing. Mr. G. got the hint and started to fan the smoke away with his cap. He realized that he was causing us discomfort and apologized but never stopped smoking. Mr. G. had his way. We resented the smoke, but we liked him too much to ask him to quit.

When the air cleared a bit he proceeded to tell us a story

about a pogrom in a small town not far from Radom that had taken place some weeks earlier. One of Mr. G.'s relatives had been an eyewitness and had managed to get away. He spoke of an elderly couple left to bleed in the middle of the town square, of broken glass, and of the plundering of Jewish shops and homes while the Polish police chief sat in a local bar pretending not to notice anything.

He sat back to sip his tea, complimented my mother on her pancakes, and, turning to my father, urged him to pack up his family and leave Poland. "Henoch, don't wait too long," he repeated over and over again. My father, calm as usual, assured him that one day soon, when the children were done with their schooling, he would do just that. This would end the discussion, at least for a while. Mr. G. would then switch the conversation to a little-known Jewish ideologue, then back to anti-Semitism, zigzagging as usual from topic to topic.

Some months later my father's business failed, and he decided to start a dry-goods store in a small community not far from Radom. We lost track of Mr. G., though I often thought about him. I commuted to my old school in Radom, and one day, on the way to the station, I caught sight of Mr. G. and decided to say hello. I ran for a whole block trying to catch up with him, finally stopping him head-on. He put his arm around me and asked me to tell my parents that he missed them. I looked at his bulging leather pouch and realized that he was getting thinner and the pouch fatter. He promised to come out and see us the following Sunday, but he never did.

The thirties drew to an end, and my father's business failed again. We moved back to Radom. Then came September 1, 1939, and World War II. Seven days later we found ourselves under Nazi occupation. It wasn't until an early spring afternoon in 1942, when we were already living in the ghetto, that Mr. G. reappeared. I spotted him entering the backyard of the little house that we shared with my grandmother and one of my aunts. He walked very slowly, with a cane. He looked emaciated; his coat was in shreds, his oversized shoes revealed bare feet, and his mustache had turned white. He wore the cap I remembered, but it had acquired a shine and now appeared to rest on his ears. I was shocked at the change but glad to see our old friend. Mr. G. called me Michael and, in a trembling voice, inquired about my parents. As it happened, my parents were inside entertaining two honored guests with a very special meal, a *chulent*—a traditional Sabbath meal consisting of stuffed derma, potatoes, kasha, and lima beans—my mother had been preparing for days. At the time it was a Herculean task to gather the ingredients for a *chulent*, as the little food available had to be purchased on the black market at exorbitant prices. My parents were indebted to these guests, and my mother had prepared the *chulent* in gratitude.

I helped Mr. G. into the kitchen and settled him in a chair next to the warm stove. He sat there staring straight into my eyes. I didn't know what to say or do. Soon the guests left; when my parents found Mr. G. in the house they were stunned. He told them that he had been ill a very long time; he couldn't remember how long. The previous day was his first out of the hospital, and he had decided to look for us. Mother made some hot tea for him, but there was no sugar left. He didn't mind, he said, for he had no teeth left. She served him a plate of what was left of the *chulent;* he cleaned the plate bit by bit without saying a word. I couldn't take my eyes off him. Then he turned to my father and, in a trembling voice, asked him if he still remembered his advice to pack up the family and leave. "I just would like you to know, Henoch, that I've been warning you all these years. You probably didn't believe me, and now it's too late, my friend." He reached for my mother's hand, kissed it, and thanked her for the "miracle meal." He called it "The last *chulent.*" He rose, and my father helped him walk back to his son's apartment, which wasn't very far; he had been staying there since his wife's death. I watched them until they turned the corner.

That was the last time I saw the tiny, shriveled Mr. G. My mother cried all evening, lamenting that there was so little she could do for him. I went out to the backyard and with all my might began to chop the little firewood that was left.

I cannot forget Mr. G. I still hear his somber farewell to my father: "Henoch, now it's too late." And every once in a while I can see him rushing by me with his bulging pouch, a tiny cigarette butt dangling from his lips.

In August, 1942, over 20,000 Jews were deported from Radom to extermination camps in the east. Mr. G. was among them.

A CHICKEN FOR
THE HOLIDAYS

At the time the Nazis occupied our city in September of 1939 my father owned a used-furniture business that he had taken over from my grandfather shortly before the war. One afternoon around October of 1940, some months before the ghetto was established, a Polish farmer came in with his wife to purchase an antique bed. They settled on a huge, very old bed with an exceedingly heavy, tall bedstead. When the time came to pay for it the couple realized they were short of money. Perhaps, my father suggested affably, they could compensate him with some provisions from their farm instead. It was agreed that one of us would visit before long— the farm was about one hour's walk from the city—to collect our debt. I happened to be present during the transaction and was introduced by my father to the farmer, Mr. Dombroski; I helped him load the bed onto his wagon. He thanked me for my help and left, obviously pleased with the acquisition.

Some months went by, but none of us ventured out to the farm. Eventually my father gave up on the idea entirely because of the danger of crossing the city limits without a proper pass, and because passes were impossible to get.

A CHICKEN FOR THE HOLIDAYS

Shortly before the Jewish High Holidays I heard my mother mention how nice it would be to have a chicken for the holidays. Immediately I thought of Mr. Dombroski's agreement with Father and started plotting a trip to the farm. I would have to walk; there was no public transportation in rural areas, and Jews were no longer allowed to ride or own bicycles under penalty of death. It was the time of martial law: no hearings, no trials, and no excuses.

I asked my Polish friend George about the safest way of walking to the Dombroskis' and if he would like to accompany me. He refused. "It's an insane idea," he told me. I even thought of asking a German soldier I knew, a client at the photo studio where I worked, if he would escort me, but I thought it to be presumptuous on my part. Although I knew how risky it was to cross the city line without a pass, alone or with a companion, I became obsessed with the idea. I wasn't going to let George or anyone else discourage me. The anticipation of adventure and the risk involved must have appealed to me, but above all I could visualize my family at the holiday dinner eyeing a cooked chicken at the center of the table. My mouth started watering at the mere thought of being able to savor a chicken giblet, as in the old days. Chickens were hard to come by and were very expensive. Open markets were banned, and farmers didn't bring their produce into town for fear of having it confiscated.

Only two days remained before the holidays. I started out on a rainy afternoon without revealing my plans to anyone— not even to my mother. The chicken was going to be a surprise. As soon as I crossed the city line, so as not to attract attention, I took off the arm band with the Star of David and briskly followed the road toward the Jewish cemetery. To be caught without the arm band was punishable by death. Soon, for safety reasons, I got off the road and walked along narrow, muddy paths or crossed pastures full of puddles. The rain intensified; the sky began to darken. Flocks of crows pecked away at the wet fields, taking off noisily at the slightest motion only to land again seconds later.

As I neared the cemetery I saw a military truck surrounded by people in uniform. Instinctively I took a detour through the woods; I had to avoid anyone in uniform at all cost. When I stopped for a moment to orient myself I realized how insane I was to be there, but I wasn't about to turn back at that point. I continued along the edge of the woods for some time until I came to a clearing covered by fog. Suddenly a salvo of rifle shots rang out from the direction of the cemetery. I stopped behind a hollow tree and virtually pressed myself into it. I was mortified.

The sky turned a dark gray; it was still raining. There was not a living soul in sight, not the slightest sound save for the wet leaves and rustling twigs underfoot; I felt as if I was alone in the world. The fog was all around me; like a procession of floating ghosts it kept spreading, enveloping every tree at the edge of the forest.

Still there was no farm in sight. Momentarily I lost my way. I wasn't sure if I really knew the country as well as I thought I did. Just then I started hearing children's voices. I stopped and turned to look, but nobody was there. I didn't think I was hallucinating, for I could still hear the voices, a whole chorus. I looked up and saw the wind-whipped treetops move in a wild dance, twirling and rotating; they were creating all sorts of weird squeaking sounds. It was eerie.

I looked at my watch; it was after six o'clock. There wasn't much time left to find the farm and get back to the city before curfew, which would begin at eight. A wild rabbit frightened me as it sped by, leaping over the brush. As I walked on I could hear the pounding of my own heart.

Some minutes later, through a thick haze, I saw the farmhouse in a clearing between the woods and a small lake surrounded by weeping willows. As I came closer to the fence a dog started barking; moments later a woman opened the door of the house. It was Mrs. Dombroski. She didn't recognize me at first, but when I told her who I was she pulled me inside.

"Oh, yes, I remember you now," she said in her high-pitched voice. "Sure, sure, I know, I know. Please come inside.

"We were wondering why no one ever showed up, so here you are. Well, my husband should be right back, and he will give you something. Maybe some fresh milk? Sit down at the table, please." I was starved and exhausted. "Thank you, ma'am," I said, and I sat down on a wooden bench. At the other end of the room I saw the huge bed they had purchased from my father, piled high with richly embroidered pillows. The bedstead reached almost to the ceiling. I was wondering what had happened to the milk Mrs. Dombroski had offered me.

Mrs. Dombroski seemed to need to talk. She moved about in her long, colorful skirt, chattering ceaselessly; everything she said, she said twice. When she finally stopped talking I asked her if I might have a live chicken.

"A live chicken?" she repeated twice after me. "And how will you carry it back to the city so that a patrol won't stop you?" she asked. "It's dangerous to carry anything live, you know. You may get arrested, or even shot. Who knows? I will be happy to give you one, but it would be easier to kill it here and take it back dead." I needed a live chicken, however, so that it could be slaughtered according to the kosher law.

"I would rather have it live," I told her stubbornly. "I can hide it under my brother's raincoat. It's a big raincoat, and there shouldn't be a problem." I didn't think I could explain that for a chicken to be kosher it would have to be slaughtered according to the laws of kashruth, for which Mrs. Dombroski couldn't be responsible.

Mr. Dombroski soon returned; after hearing me out he decided to let me have a live chicken. In the event I was stopped, he said, it would be my responsibility.

"You are not to tell anyone where you got the chicken. Chances are that you could be accused of having stolen it, which would only make matters worse," he said.

Finally Mrs. Dombroski gave me a tin cup of fresh milk and a thick slice of home-baked bread. I hadn't had fresh milk in months, and the bread tasted like cake. When I thanked her for her hospitality she just waved her hand at me, saying, "I would like to give you more, but I'm afraid too much fresh milk would make you sick." Then she went out, to return with a gray-yellow bird, not very big, with scared eyes. It kept turning its head nervously without making a sound. She had tied its feet and wings with straps of cloth to prevent its escape. The chicken fit under my raincoat with its feet tied behind my belt; I would have to support it with my left hand through the raincoat pocket. The Dombroskis silently stuffed my empty pockets with bread and potatoes, and Mr. Dombroski walked me to the road. I must have looked ridiculous loaded down with so many provisions.

"If they catch you," Mr. Dombroski said, "you don't know me, and I don't know you." "I won't tell a thing," I assured him. "And don't forget to tell your father that we're even. The chicken is worth much more than I owe him." He wished me luck and went back to his house. I took a shortcut, bypassing the woods, and trudged along a narrow, muddy road. I feared that I might not be able to make it back on time if I was to return through the woods; in any event, my shoes were covered with thick mud, and my feet were wet and cold.

It was past dusk; the visibility was bad. The whole landscape seemed to be drowning in the rain, which had long since penetrated every inch of my raincoat. A farmer drove by, his horse and wagon splashing me with mud. The chicken kept quiet, and it kept me warm, and as I got closer to the city line the fog started to lift, exposing the contours of a row of low-lying houses. I leaned against a tree to rest and slipped on my arm band. I realized I was just as scared wearing the arm band as I was without it.

By the time I crossed the city line it was almost dark. At a street intersection a German soldier in an SS uniform emerged from a house and blocked my way. I stopped and recognized him immediately: It was Schultz, a Pole-Volksdeutsch of German descent who had volunteered for the Waffen SS. Some weeks before he had come to the studio to be photographed, and I had taken care of him.

"Where are you off to at this hour?" he asked me.

"I'm on my way home after visiting a sick friend, sir," I lied. "I just realized how close it is to curfew. By the way, I do remember you from the photo studio," I added very casually. Suddenly I felt the chicken move. I wanted only for it to keep quiet; it would have been disastrous had Schultz discovered a chicken under my raincoat.

"Yes, yes, I remember you, too," Schultz answered impatiently, waving me off. "Now hurry home," he yelled. I didn't have to be told twice; I had never walked so fast before.

As soon as I left Schultz the chicken grew restless and noisy; I thought it must have been scared by the SS man's yelling. I tried to caress it with my free hand; I held its beak, but nothing helped. I was desperate; the walk back was the most risky of all, and I knew there was no turning back. I remembered a story my grandmother had told me years before about a young peasant girl who in the middle of the night got lost in the woods while looking for a doctor to attend her sick mother, and who in desperation asked God to guide her.

"Please, God, help me, too, and keep this chicken quiet," I started praying under my breath. "I must get this chicken home alive so we can celebrate the holidays. Please make it keep quiet."

For the next few moments I thought God had heard me. The chicken was silent, though not for very long. Suddenly she let out a loud, attention-getting cluck; fortunately there were no pedestrians in earshot. The streets were nearly deserted.

"Dear God," I continued, "how can you let this chicken jeopardize my life? Please get us home safely. My family is waiting for me."

The chicken's clucking was getting louder. I panicked, tightened my grip around the chicken's neck, and held on until the bird quieted. I felt its legs moving up from behind my belt, its whole body stiffening as if it was trying to free itself. I felt awful.

Just then I saw a German police patrol on the opposite side of the street, walking in my direction. I hid inside the gate of a building until they passed, but they stopped directly across from me to talk to a woman. It was eight minutes before curfew. I broke out in a new sweat. Should I leave the dead chicken in the yard and climb some fences so as to get home faster? Or should I wait a bit longer? After a minute I looked out again, but the patrol was still there with the woman, pointing now at the building in which I was hiding. I was trapped.

Without giving it another thought, with the little strength still left in me, I pulled myself over the fence behind me, the dead chicken dangling from my belt, and sped off through yards and orchards, climbing more fences, some lined with barbed wire, until I reached our street. A friendly stray dog came close, sniffing at the chicken. He followed me to the gate of our building, where I was greeted by a long line of German soldiers waiting their turn at Stasia's whorehouse. Stasia was an enterprising Polish woman who—with the help of the German authorities—had taken over three adjoining sheds, evicting the tenants and converting the sheds to a pleasure house catering exclusively to the German army.

"Wie gehts dier?" one of them asked in a sort of friendly tone of voice. *"Danke, sehr gut, mein Herr,"* I answered, and I ran home.

It was past curfew by the time I got to our apartment. My worried mother stood at the door waiting for me. "Where were you?" she demanded with tears in her eyes. "Why all this mud all over you? Did you know how many arrests and executions for curfew violations there are every night?"

As soon as I entered the apartment I pulled out the dead chicken and deposited it on the doormat, as if in explanation.

"I'm sorry, Mother, but the chicken had to be strangled," I said. "It was making too much noise."

A CHICKEN FOR THE HOLIDAYS

"Where did you get a chicken?" Mother asked.

When I told her the whole story tears started running down her face. She came closer to embrace me and held me in her arms. I could feel her tears on my neck, behind my shirt collar, and the strength of her caring arms. It gave me a jolt of renewed self-confidence, moving me to tears.

"I think what you did was extraordinary," Mother said, "and all thanks to the Almighty for bringing you back alive. You committed no crime, and you must promise me never to risk your life again. We would survive even if it meant having a meatless holiday."

"It wasn't very risky," I lied to her. "No one stopped me, and it was nice to be out in the country, even though it rained a lot." "But now," Mother was saying, "I'm sorry to tell you that in spite of the risk you have taken to make this a better holiday for all of us, we can't eat an unkosher chicken. We'll probably give it to the janitor's family. It would be a shame to throw it away."

"But Mother," I interrupted, "it's wartime, and there's a food shortage. Does it really matter that the chicken isn't kosher? Who'll know? Won't God forgive us?" I pleaded with her, but Mother was unrelenting. "In wartime or peacetime," Mother answered, "we're a people who must abide by the laws, or else we'll cease to be a people. That's the best explanation I can give. But let me assure you that you're a dear son, and I'll always love you."

The chicken went to the janitor's family; weeks later his wife was still talking about it, reminding my mother what a tasty and fat bird it had been.

ALEXANDRA

One early morning during the winter of 1940 I was sitting at my desk in the photo studio, looking through some receipts, when I heard a rattle at the glass-paneled door. I opened it to find a young woman dressed in a tweed coat and a woolen cap; she came in quickly, closing the door behind her. Her face was round and red-cheeked, her eyes as green as turquoise.

She apologized for having caused so much noise at the door. "Think nothing of it," I told her. "The glass is shaky, and we can't get anybody to fix it."

"This war makes everything shake," she answered. "I need a picture in a hurry for an ID card. Could you possibly do it by tomorrow morning?" I assured her that I could, and at no extra cost, and asked her to come into the studio.

She took off her cap, and two long braids tumbled down, reaching to her hips. Her hair was brown and smoothly combed back from her forehead. She took off her coat and, positioning herself before the studio mirror, began rearranging her braids. She wrapped them twice around her head, pinning the ends at the back; the result was that she seemed to be wearing a crown. She wore no makeup, but her lips were

48

full and red, the color of a rose. Her high cheekbones were perfectly symmetrical, and her eyebrows were equally arched.

I was in awe. Never before had I seen such a lovely face so near. I felt pangs in my stomach. So stunned that I could think of nothing to say, I got to work. I took several exposures to make sure I didn't make a mistake; my subject gave me her name, paid for the pictures, and promised to come back for the prints the following morning.

I was restless and could hardly get through the day. Before the afternoon was over the pictures were ready and waiting inside the desk drawer. I made an extra print for myself and stuck it in my wallet; every few minutes I would take it out and look at it. My coworkers wondered aloud about my uncharacteristic absentmindedness, and Mrs. Orenstein, the owner's wife, sent me many curious glances.

I had heard all kinds of stories about people falling deeply in love but wasn't particularly familiar with the subject; all I knew was that when I thought about Alexandra my heart started pounding. I remembered a story my Uncle Joe had once told me about how he had fallen in love when he was my age, almost seventeen. He had loved the girl secretly and never let her know his feelings. He called it a "platonic" love. In the end she married someone else; when Uncle Joe found out about it he was heartbroken and decided never to get married. But some years later he changed his mind, marrying my Aunt Natalie. Did he carry a grudge against his first love? I asked him. "No, not at all," he assured me. He was only sorry that he hadn't been brave enough at the time to express his feelings.

I thought about Uncle Joe's unfortunate love story most of the evening and assured myself I would let Alexandra know very soon how I felt about her. I was even tempted to ask my parents how they had fallen in love, but I didn't think they would be willing to discuss the subject. They were very bashful and always guarded their privacy.

That night I could hardly sleep. I took Alexandra's picture to bed with me, and in the middle of the night, flashlight in hand, I studied it. My bed was in the kitchen, and no one in the apartment could see what I was doing. I must have fallen asleep; when I woke in the morning the German tenants with whom the housing authorities had asked us to share our apartment were already in the kitchen preparing their breakfast. They were pointing at the picture; I had been holding onto it in my sleep.

I got up in a hurry, and after gulping down some hot chicory coffee I dressed and left the apartment. It was cold, and the frozen ground was covered with a thick coat of snow that had fallen during the night. Slipping and falling, I made it to the studio. I cleaned the snow off the padlock, removed the iron crossbar, and opened both the outer double doors and the faulty glass-paneled entrance door.

It was still quite early. I took out Alexandra's pictures and, arranging them side by side, studied them. I was sitting there daydreaming when the door opened very quietly and closed with even less noise. I heard Alexandra's greeting. She stopped at the desk and grinned. She wore a fluffy fur hat that made her look even more beautiful than the woolen cap she had worn the day before; the green of her eyes was even more striking. I tried to gather up the three pictures in a hurry, but the envelope fell to the floor, and when I bent down to retrieve it I banged my head against the desk. It was very embarrassing, and for Alexandra very amusing, I thought.

"I want to thank you for being so punctual," she said. "The picture is much better than I expected; after all, it's only for an ID card. The way it looks, I should really have it enlarged and give it to my relatives. It's a decent photograph, don't you think?"

"I certainly do," I remember saying, not very sure of myself. Alexandra noticed my shyness and tried to help me. She ordered some enlargements and inquired when she could bring her little niece in to be photographed. "Any time at all," I assured her, and she extended her hand. I took it and pressed it gently, feeling the smoothness of her skin. It felt as if I were touching silk. Although afraid of chafing it with my rough hand, chapped from mixing chemicals, I was reluctant to let go of it; if I only had the courage to cover it with kisses and tell her how I felt about her. Uncle Joe's story flashed through my mind. Why don't I tell her? I kept thinking while she put on her mittens.

Alexandra smiled, bade me good-bye, and walked out, promising to come back the following week. In a daze I watched her leave, hating myself for being such a coward. By now my coworkers were arriving, and the studio was getting busy. German soldiers, some of them armed with rifles or pistols, came in with film to be processed, talking loudly to one another, complaining about the cold weather. They stamped the snow off their boots onto the floor of the reception room and loosened their heavy belts. One of them started eating a sandwich loaded with thick slices of pink ham that hung down over the crusts of the bread. The sight of it made me hungry; I hadn't tasted ham since the war started. Meat of any kind was rare, to be had only on the black market at exorbitant prices. The heavy aroma of disinfectant followed the soldiers, and after a while the whole studio smelled like a hospital ward. I lost myself in everyday chores but continued to feel Alexandra's smooth hand against mine. I smelled my hand and discovered a faint scent of carnation. She must use a scented soap, I thought; it couldn't be perfume. There were no perfumes available; only the Nazis had them. I didn't think Alexandra was the type to associate with the Nazis.

Nearly a week went by. One morning after a heavy snowfall Alexandra arrived with her little niece, whose name was Kasia. She was a beautiful youngster with an angelic face, and she turned out to be very friendly. I showed them into the studio and turned on the electric heater. There was a severe coal shortage, and firewood was being sold at a premium. I placed Kasia in Alexandra's lap, and that was how I photographed them: Alexandra in her fur hat towering over the little blond head, the little girl looking straight at the camera, smiling. I didn't know what to say and kept searching for words, taking deep breaths and stealing glances at Alexandra. Too soon they were getting ready to leave; again I was treated to a silken handshake. Kasia kissed me good-bye on my cheek.

Mr. Orenstein, the studio proprietor, wanted to know why I took so much time in the studio. "There's a long line of soldiers waiting to be photographed. These aren't pictures for a contest," he reminded me. "You're taking too much time."

A couple of days later Alexandra came back to look at the proofs. Unexpectedly she arrived late in the afternoon instead of in the morning. Hardly anyone was left in the studio when she came in. I showed her to the workroom behind the office, which was warmer and cozier than the rest of the place. Soon we were alone. I was overwhelmed by her presence; this time I promised myself to tell her how I felt about her. As soon as I sat down next to her, however, I forgot what I wanted to say. The scent of carnations was intoxicating.

A gas burner glowed on top of the worktable, and the flame reflected in her eyes. The hissing of the flame was the only sound I could hear; in my desperation to find a topic for conversation I was getting stomach cramps. I stole a glimpse of the contour of her breasts through her tight sweater. It was a tempting sight—it reminded me of the torso of a mannequin I used to see in a window advertising ladies' wear. Suddenly I remembered that Alexandra wanted to see her proofs. I retrieved them from the bin and handed them to her.

Alexandra looked at the proofs, told me how much she liked them, and selected some. Before I had a chance to thank her she moved closer and, almost in a whisper, said, "There's something I would like to ask you, if I may." "Please do," I answered. "Well," she began, "it's something rather important, and it could be dangerous, but I have a feeling you're the right person. Working in a photo studio, you have many opportunities to see all kinds of photos that the Nazis drop off to process, am I right?" I nodded in agreement. I was afraid to make a sound. "There're some people," she continued, "who would be interested in getting hold of some extra copies of those photos. One day they could save some other people's lives." After a short pause she added, "It sounds strange, doesn't it?"

I was stunned. Then she reached for my hand and made me promise that, whatever my decision, her words would stay between us. "It could be very dangerous to talk about this," she said.

Thoroughly intoxicated by her closeness, I moved my mouth toward hers and found her lips. She responded in kind. I knew then that I didn't have to tell her how I felt about her. We were out of breath, and I was only sorry that we wouldn't remain so forever. It was time to close the studio; Alexandra stood up. Her green eyes sparkled like two twinkling lanterns reflecting on a lake. She came closer and whispered, "We'll be good friends, I can tell." Before I had turned from getting my coat out of the closet she was gone.

After that my life changed drastically. In the chaos and confusion of everyday chores I saw a purpose in living, and not just a struggle for survival. As much as I liked to work at the studio (which protected me against being sent to a labor camp, after all), Alexandra and her cause became the center of my existence. I was ready to offer my life to her and her cause.

A few days later she showed up in the company of a young, handsome man, whom she introduced as her brother. His name was Lech; he wanted to talk to me privately, soon, and not at the studio, he said. He let himself be photographed so as not to cause any suspicions, and he played the part of a customer. He kept studying me while I photographed him, which made me uneasy.

Several blocks away from the studio lived Alexandra's sister, Joanna, with her husband and little Kasia. The following evening after work I met Lech at her apartment. I took an oath, a vow of silence, and thus became another link in the active chain of the Polish underground. My job was to secure photos of high-ranking officials of the Gestapo and of any other German agency associated with the governing of Poland. Procedures were established for the passing on of photos; signals were agreed upon in case of a slip-up. Nothing that was said that evening was to be written down, and all vital information had to be memorized. Above all, I was told never to speak to anyone unless they knew the password. In case of a confrontation with the Gestapo, I had never met any of these people, including Alexandra. Also, I was instructed to destroy the negatives from Alexandra's ID-card photo. I listened intently and tried to remember every word I heard. It was almost curfew by the time we had finished; I raced out into the snowy street and, running, made it home on time.

Mr. Orenstein, the owner of the studio, had been retouching negatives for the Gestapo for some time. The glass-plate negatives had to be picked up from the Gestapo twice a week, brought to the studio, and, when ready, returned to the Gestapo. I was the one who shuttled the negatives back and forth. Soon I decided to make quick prints before turning over the negatives to Mr. Orenstein. The system worked, and before long I had accumulated almost fifty photos, which I hid in the studio on the floor of a closet, covered with boxes of old negatives. In addition I managed to lift pictures of atrocities and executions; German soldiers had photographed them and brought us the film to process. I developed a technique of lifting pictures that went on as long as the studio was in existence—that is, until late summer, 1942.

Alexandra would show up once a week under the pretext of ordering pictures of herself or her relatives or bringing an old picture to copy, and I would transfer all the stolen pictures to her. She never told me where those pictures went; curious as I was to know, I never dared ask. I trusted her and was ready to do anything she would ask of me. In the early spring of 1941 a ghetto was established, and things began to get difficult. Unexpected roundups of young people became a norm; anyone without a job was a target. I was still employed at the studio and had a special pass that allowed me to leave the ghetto and be protected from roundups.

One evening just before closing time Alexandra showed up. She assured me that some people would keep an eye on me, and that I would be safe; in case of trouble they would rescue me. They had the means, she said. "Why should they do such a thing?" I inquired. "Because you're one of us, and you're valuable," she answered. I looked at her in disbelief. What a shame that I couldn't share this news with my mother; how proud she would have been. I came closer to Alexandra and touched her cheek. She closed her eyes, and I kissed her eyelids. Her lashes fluttered quickly, nervously. I inhaled her fresh scent and felt as if I were floating on a bed of flowers.

I heard someone at the front door. Leaving Alexandra in the workroom, I went out to find a Nazi gendarme who was there to pick up his processed film. When I handed it to him he pulled out some prints; he smiled when he saw them. Holding two in front of me, he commented, "He won't do it again." They were pictures of an execution, taken at very close range. My knees began to shake; I had lifted some copies of those photos. He paid his bill, gave me a pack of cigarettes, and left.

"I'll be gone for a while, and you shouldn't worry about me," Alexandra announced when I returned. "My sister Joanna will be your contact while I'm gone." Suppose she doesn't come back, I thought, and if she does, I might not be here. As she was getting ready to leave a sadness descended upon me. To miss a person one cares for can be torture, but to worry about a person's safety is a cruel punishment.

Several weeks went by, and neither Alexandra nor Joanna showed up. I wasn't supposed to inquire about or search for Alexandra at all. I just had to learn to be patient and wait. I thought that perhaps she had changed her mind about a relationship with a Jew and decided not to see me again. It was very risky for a Christian to be in contact with a Jew, and punishable with imprisonment if discovered. I tried to resign myself to never seeing her again.

I kept lifting more pictures, hiding them inside a metal box under the darkroom floor. The old hiding place was too risky; too many people were using the big closet. I was a nervous wreck. As soon as I started hearing rumors about a deportation I took the pictures to Joanna's apartment. They were too valuable to destroy. Joanna was shocked to see me but quickly accepted the pictures. "It's very risky what you're doing," she told me. "Don't ever drop off anything to anybody without specific instructions." I knew she was annoyed at me.

Meantime a deportation took place, the ghetto was reduced substantially, and the photo studio was closed. I found employment with another studio owned by a Polish couple of German extraction; I was escorted to the studio every morning and back to the ghetto every evening by a cop.

Some weeks later a man appeared at the back door of the studio and asked for me. We went out to the yard, and he introduced himself. "My name is Victor," he said. It was the first time I had heard the password. "Alexandra sent me to tell you that she is well and will be here next month. Now, I need two pictures of you for a new ID card, and I must have it in two days at most. Is there anything you need?" Not being able to think of anything, I blurted out, "I just lost my mother in the deportation." "I'm sorry. I lost my mother when I was five," he answered, squeezing my shoulder. He left quickly; somewhat confused, I went back to the studio. Alexandra remembered me; she must care, I told myself.

Two days later Victor came back to get the pictures; shortly after he brought my new ID card. My new name was Bronislaw Godlewski; my initials remained unchanged. I couldn't possibly carry the card with me, nor could I leave it in the ghetto for fear of unexpected searches. My picture was on it, and it would be easy to find me. To own a forged ID was punishable by death. In case I decided to hide outside the ghetto, my forged identity card would be of value, but to carry it around inside was extremely risky. I slipped it inside the lining of my hat; I had nightmares every time I went to sleep or hung up my hat at the studio. The ID card alone made me a nervous wreck.

The winter wasn't letting up. Snow fell incessantly, and temperatures stayed below the zero mark for weeks on end. One afternoon during a blizzard I heard a faint tapping at the studio windowpane. I looked out to see Alexandra, her hat covered with snow. I ran out as fast as I could, my heart pounding, and embraced her right there in the middle of the blizzard. We walked into the hallway behind the staircase and continued to embrace. I covered her wet face with kisses and tasted her salty tears. In my delirium I whispered into her ear, "If you only knew how much I missed you." She didn't speak. She reached for her shoulder bag and took out a package. "Here," she said. "I knitted a scarf and a sweater for you." I was in awe. I pulled the sweater on, and she wrapped the scarf around my neck. It felt soft and fluffy, and a warm feeling filled my whole being. I took her hands and covered them with kisses.

A man came down the staircase. Passing us by, he stopped for a few seconds to curse at the weather. He looked at us, pulled his hat down over his ears, and went outside, still complaining about the cold.

I couldn't let go of Alexandra. Streaks of melted snow were running off her fur hat, and the water was leaving wet patches on her coat. She held the ends of my scarf against her cheeks. "Now listen," she began. "We have a plan to get you out of here. Next Monday Lech will be here with a car at dusk, before quitting time. He'll stop at the gate on Traugutta Street with the engine running. You'll probably see him from your window. Leave by the back door and walk slowly toward the gate. When you get close Lech will open the door from the inside, and you'll hop in quickly. Don't carry anything with you but a toothbrush, and have your ID in your pocket, not inside your hat. The trip will be safe because Lech has all the necessary papers, and he speaks German fluently."

How lucky I was to have Alexandra for a friend, I thought. I imagined being hidden deep inside a thick forest, away from the Nazis and their spies, who were constantly on the prowl for hidden Jews. How would I ever be able to repay her? A jolt of happiness went through me; thinking about the rescue filled me with excitement.

Alexandra came by once more to see me; she brought me

some sweet rolls her sister had baked. She wanted to say good-bye before Monday's escape. She was going to Warsaw by train and soon would come to visit me in my hideout, not far from Warsaw. It was the beginning of November, 1943; the Germans were retreating after their defeat at Stalingrad, and the whole picture was changing rapidly. "The war can't go on much longer," Alexandra told me, "and the underground needs every able-bodied man and woman." I stood at the entrance to the hallway, hypnotized by her beauty. She threw me a kiss before disappearing behind the gate.

Monday arrived only slowly; I spent most of the day at my retouching stand in the studio, watching the window and studying my coworkers' expressions. Did they suspect me of anything? There had been rumors for days that the Nazis were planning another deportation. Did they sense my desperation? When dusk came, and with it a light snowfall, my stomach felt like a tight knot. Suddenly I heard the roar of an engine. I looked out and saw a black Ford at the gate. I reacted immediately, which was probably the wrong thing to do. Before I could reach the back door one of my coworkers let out a loud scream, which stopped me cold. I decided not to run. It could cause a commotion and put Lech in danger. Mr. Skonecny, the owner, came running, knocked me to the ground, and sat on top of me until the escorting cop arrived to take me back to the ghetto.

I'm sure Lech waited as long as he could. He must have realized that something had gone wrong and left. The following day at dawn the remainder of the ghetto was surrounded; some hours later I was in a cattle car on my way to Maidanek. I carried my forged ID card into the camp, ripped it to bits in the shower room, and watched it go down the drain. Bronislaw Godlewski ceased to exist, never having lived.

As soon as the war was over I went back to my home town to look for Alexandra. Her sister wasn't living at the same address any longer. "She's moved," the janitor informed me, though he didn't know where. Did he know her sister Alexandra? I asked. I tried to describe her looks, the color of her eyes, but he wasn't interested and resumed sweeping the walk. Very abruptly he said, "I never heard of anybody by that name, and furthermore I have been here just a few months."

It was raining, and the chilly air penetrated my wet coat. Instinctively I started walking along Zeromskiego Street and went into the courtyard where the photo studio had been. The yard was gray and depressing, and there was hardly anyone in sight. A strong longing for Alexandra almost moved me to tears. Inside the entrance gate, on the wall behind a pane of glass, I saw a list of tenants; at the top of the list was a name like Alexandra's sister's, Baranska. I couldn't imagine it was possible. Could it be the same person? Without a moment's hesitation I ran up the stairs and knocked at the door. I was covered with gooseflesh by the time I heard a voice from behind the door. "Who is it?" asked a high-pitched female voice I didn't recognize. "A friend, please open," I answered. Could it be Alexandra? I wondered. I wasn't sure what Alexandra's voice sounded like. I heard the door being unlatched, and then a key turning in the lock; slowly the door came slightly ajar, and I recognized Alexandra's sister, Joanna.

The hallway where I stood was dark, and her pale, drawn face stood out sharply in the dim light. I apologized, mumbling the most incomprehensible words while extending my arm to greet her. She opened the door wider and asked me inside. "What a surprise, how nice to see you," she said, taking my wet raincoat from me while showing me to the sitting room. "You haven't changed a bit. Perhaps you're somewhat thinner . . . but I know you were taken to camp, and believe me, we prayed for you. I just came back from taking Kasia to school. I am sure she would have loved to see you. Won't you have some tea? Please sit down and rest. I must talk to you." My mind was numbed by one question only: Where was Alexandra?

"Forgive me for the messy apartment," I heard her say.

"And please call me Joanna. No formalities. After all, we are old friends." She went to the kitchen to prepare the tea, and I was left alone in the room. On a bookshelf I saw a framed photograph of Alexandra and Kasia; it was the one I had taken during the war. I stood up to look at it closely and then walked over to the window. The photo studio had been on the opposite side of the building, closer to the gate. Through the fogged-up window I could see a faint outline of its entrance dissolving behind the raindrops. I was transfixed. This is where I met Alexandra, I thought. It all seemed unreal. Four years had gone by.

Joanna came in with the tea and put it on top of a small table next to the window. "Please sit down," she insisted. I wasn't able to hold my anxiety at bay any longer and said point-blank, "Tell me, where is Alexandra?"

Joanna seemed to be startled by the sudden question. After a brief silence she said sadly, looking into my eyes: "You know, life is full of ironies. You were the one in constant danger, and Alexandra always worried about you. However, the one thing she was sure of, she told me, was that you'd come back. She was right. You came back and she didn't."

KURT

On a wet morning during the winter of 1941 a tall, lean soldier with high cheekbones and light brown eyes came into the photo studio where I worked. The lapels of his tunic were adorned with insignia of the Waffen SS; on his hat was a round black patch with a silver skull and crossbones. Around his waist he wore a black leather belt from which hung a bayonet in a green metal sheath. The sight of him sent shivers down my spine.

In a hardly audible voice he greeted me with a prolonged *"Guuten Morgen"* and asked me if I spoke German. "Somewhat," I answered. He then took off his gloves and energetically began to wipe his muddy boots on the decaying doormat until it split in two. When I asked him to have a seat he thanked me politely and walked over to inspect a display of photographs on one of the reception-room walls.

As soon as I had finished with the other customers—all of them German soldiers—I asked the SS man if I could be of help to him. "Yes," he told me, speaking softly, almost apologetically. "I would like to be photographed." His name was Kurt, he told me, and he insisted that was all the name I needed. Soon after he was photographed, realizing that we were alone in the reception room, he turned abruptly to ask, "Could you tell me the meaning of the *Kommissarische Leitung* sign displayed over this establishment?" I was surprised by his naïve question; everyone knew full well what *Kommissarische Leitung* meant.

"This used to be a Jewish-owned business," I answered dutifully. "It was taken over recently by the German state, and it's being administered by a trustee, with the former owner as an employee."

As soon as I finished my explanation he told me how impressed he was with my knowledge of the German language. "You speak much better than I expected. And you," he asked, "are you a Jew?"

"Yes, I am," I answered, somewhat frightened. Quickly he reached inside the canvas pouch he carried under his arm and pulled out a small loaf of bread. "Please take this, it's for you," he said. I was surprised and thanked him for it; as I turned to put it with my things behind the desk two German officers came in. Kurt gave them a Nazi salute and left. I didn't know what to think of such an act of generosity, especially on the part of an SS man.

I didn't stop to think that there might be something wrong with the bread; I only wondered why Kurt had given it to me. How could I turn down food under any circumstances? We were hungry.

When I took home the bread that evening and told my parents about Kurt they thought the entire incident highly suspect. They warned me to be cautious and not to ask the SS man for anything. I assured them that I hadn't, that he had given me the loaf of bread of his own volition.

A few days after Kurt was photographed he came back to the studio to place his photo order. He seemed to linger after he had done so; as soon as the reception room emptied he gave me a tightly packed canvas pouch full of food. I was reluctant to take it and wanted to reimburse him for it, but he refused to accept any money. We had a fairly long conversation about camera techniques and films, but he volunteered nothing about himself. He liked to take pictures of landscapes, he told me, but still had difficulties getting the right exposures. Then he asked me all about life in the ghetto, and about my family.

"One day when this war is over," Kurt said, "we'll have a long talk. Not now; it may be dangerous."

At the time my grandmother was recovering from a stroke and needed a medication that wasn't available at any of the local apothecaries. Some days after, as a last resort, I asked Kurt if he might obtain some; the following day he brought a supply large enough to last for weeks. Again he refused even to discuss compensation, saying, "This is the least I could do for your sick grandmother."

Soon after Kurt brought a picture of his own grandmother into the studio and ordered a copy of it for his wallet. Many German soldiers would bring their old family photos to be copied so that they could carry them in their wallets. Looking at the picture after he had gone, I realized that there was nothing typically Germanic about his grandmother; for one reason or another I made an extra print and took it home to show it to my parents. They were astonished to see that Kurt's grandmother was dark-eyed and had Semitic features. "She looks so Jewish," my mother commented. From then on my parents speculated frequently on Kurt's origins. My mother insisted—given his irregular behavior—that there had to be a Jewish connection; thereafter Kurt became "the Jewish SS man."

Some weeks went by without a visit from Kurt. I worried that someone had seen him giving me food and had denounced him to the Gestapo. I had heard of a similar case in which a German soldier had been helping a Jewish woman and her child with food; he was betrayed, charged with *Rassenschande* (violation of the Nuremberg racial laws), court-martialed, and sentenced to a hard-labor camp. Kurt's disappearance became one more of our daily concerns. Quite often I could hear my mother say, "I hope Kurt didn't get in trouble for helping Jews."

Quite unexpectedly, toward the end of May, 1942, after an absence of over a year, Kurt showed up again. He arrived early one morning, soon after I had opened the studio. I hardly recognized him. He was pale and thin, and obviously in poor health. As my eyes adjusted to the dim light of the reception-room corner where he stood I realized that the left sleeve of his jacket was tucked into his belt, and that there was no arm inside it. He greeted me in a shaky voice; pointing to his sleeve, he said, "Wars aren't much fun, but I still have my right arm."

I wanted to let him know how sorry I was about his arm, but I wasn't sure if I should. I felt awkward; being a Jew hardly allowed me such intimacy with a member of the *Herrenfolk*. If only he hadn't been wearing that dreadful uniform, things would have been different; my worst nightmares involved men dressed in uniforms like Kurt's. Still, afraid as I was, I was curious about how and where he had lost his arm.

Kurt started talking. "They want me to get an artificial arm," he said, "but I would rather not have one. I can live with one arm; it's probably safer that way. I won't have to go back to the Russian front," he said, smiling sadly.

I wasn't sure what he was implying. Could a man in an SS uniform possibly be against the war? I was confused; I couldn't figure him out.

Kurt inquired about my family; as usual he produced a voluminous bag of food. I begged him to accept some form of payment, but he wouldn't hear of it.

"Take it," he insisted. "Your family must be hungry, and I have too much to eat."

As soon as the reception room started to fill up Kurt took out some film, which he left for processing. As he turned toward the door he threw a Nazi salute to one of the officers in the reception room. I could see him leaving through the glass-paneled door; he wore a funny smile on his face. I wondered whether his Nazi salute wasn't a fake.

That evening I told my parents about Kurt's reappearance. They blessed him for his deeds and wished him good health. I was afraid that Kurt was perhaps overdoing things, and so as not to arouse any suspicions I decided to stop accepting food parcels from him.

August of 1942 began with an unusual heat wave. Before long rumors started circulating about deportations. Some months back we had heard dreadful accounts of deportations at the Warsaw ghetto, but very few people were willing to believe the same could happen in our own city. By the time we realized otherwise it was too late. Two consecutive deportations took place that summer, and out of twenty-eight thousand people not quite five thousand remained. We were squeezed into an area consisting of three narrow streets of two-story houses.

After the deportations Kurt returned once more to the studio. He wanted to know if I was still there and what had happened to my family. He told me how sorry he was about my mother's deportation and my grandmother's death; I was afraid to tell him that my grandmother had been shot. "The war won't last much longer," he said. He asked me to draw a diagram of the house in the ghetto where I lived. I hesitated at first, but, not wanting to make him feel as if I distrusted him, I finally drew the diagram. That night I had nightmares about being arrested by the Gestapo and shipped off to a camp.

The following week the studio itself was confiscated. I lost my job and my contact with Kurt, though soon I was hired by another studio owned by a Polish couple of German descent. They were given permission by the *Polizeiführer* to employ three Jews; I was one of them.

On a cold, rainy Sunday morning several weeks after we were moved into a smaller ghetto a neighbor came rushing to our door to tell me a German soldier outside the ghetto fence was asking for me. "He sounds as if he knows you," my neighbor reported. It would have to be Kurt, I thought, somewhat frightened. I went out and, to my astonishment, found him on the other side of the fence. As soon as he saw me he yelled, *"Aufpassen"*—watch out—and threw a bag over the fence in my direction. Before I had a chance to pick up the bag another one landed at my feet. It was daring of him. I wondered if he knew that not very far up the street stood a German police station, and that patrols along the fence were quite frequent.

I walked closer to the fence to thank him and to urge him to leave. *"Danke sehr, fielen dank"*—thank you, thank you very much—I kept repeating. "You shouldn't have done it. It's dangerous," I told him, a teenage boy advising an SS man.

"Auf Wiedersehen, mein Freund," I heard him say as he shrugged and turned to cross the street. As I watched him go a German police patrol appeared from around the corner; when he saw the patrol he quickly raised his good arm and yelled the Nazi salute at the top of his lungs.

I didn't see Kurt again until one day toward the end of the following year, when the ghetto was dissolved. I marched toward the train that would take us away one freezing afternoon; there was Kurt, rifle slung over his shoulder, in a long line of SS men standing guard. He had two arms; he must have gotten an artificial limb after all. Before boarding the cattle car I filed past him at a fairly close distance. I hoped he would notice me, but he wasn't looking in my direction. He was looking at the sky instead, as if trying to ignore what was happening around him.

It was snowing when the train started moving. I pushed my way closer to the door; through the crack I could see Kurt's silhouette getting smaller and smaller until it dissolved behind a thick screen of snowflakes. I was in a rage. I wanted to scream, just to let him know that this was probably the last time he would ever see me. Soon it got dark. Exhausted and hungry, I slipped to the floor of the moving car. I can still remember the monotonous knocking of the wheels against the track seams, the arguments people were having over space in the overcrowded car, but mostly I remember my own fury over whether Kurt had seen me get on that train.

The following morning, to my surprise, I recognized Leon, my brother's friend. He sat on the floor at the far end of the car. When I called his name he came over to join me at the door, and for the rest of the trip we stood up talking. We hadn't seen each other for over two years, since the creation of the ghetto, and there was a lot to talk about.

Many years ago, when the war was over but his image was still fresh in my memory, I tried to look for Kurt. I didn't get very far. I had never known either his last name or where he came from. All I remembered was that he was tall and lean, that he wore a long green military tunic with SS insignia on his lapels, and that he was charitable and good at heart.

HELMUT
REINER

On a very beautiful Sunday afternoon in August of 1942 a heavyset man dressed in a Gestapo uniform, fully armed and wearing a steel helmet, left the Radom ghetto escorting a man and a woman and a sickly-looking little boy. He had a full, massive face with broad jawbones and light blue eyes; his name was Helmut Reiner. His expression was extremely serious, as if he was trying to add an air of formality to his mission. Heavy beads of perspiration rolled down his face onto his neck, dripping under the collar of his woolen tunic. Clearly he hadn't thought to loosen the collar; to do so would be against regulations.

Leaving the ghetto, Reiner turned to the right, heading north toward Żeromskiego Street. His steps—in heavy boots with reinforced soles—echoed metallically against the rows of low-lying tenements.

The couple under escort, perhaps in their thirties, were the Orensteins, a highly skilled local photographer and his wife. They appeared agitated. They were dressed lightly; on their left arms they wore white arm bands with blue Stars of David.

As the boy couldn't keep up with the fast pace of the adults, his father soon stooped to carry him along.

Orenstein had strong features, and his scarred eye, the result of a childhood accident, added a certain severity to his looks. He was well built, of medium height, and his pitch-black hair was neatly combed and parted on the left side. With his free arm he carried a small suitcase; a faded green knapsack was strapped to his back. The perspiration running down his forehead nearly blinded him, but he had no way of wiping it away; he was clearly interested in getting away from the ghetto as fast as he possibly could.

The somewhat plump Mrs. Orenstein wore a flowery dress and a beige raincoat. She had on high-heeled shoes, which made it more difficult for her to walk on the cobblestone streets. There was fear in her eyes, but every now and then she would smile faintly at the boy to reassure him that all was well.

The little boy sat in the crook of his father's arm, holding tightly to his neck. He was clearly unwell; his skin seemed to have turned a yellowish green. Only when he saw a woman with a dog come out of a building did his face light up; one never saw dogs in the ghetto.

The four continued in the heat along Żeromskiego Street, away from the ghetto. Few pedestrians stopped to look; since the deportations had begun one saw Jews escorted in and out of the ghetto quite often.

Most of the day truckloads of SS and Ukrainian auxiliary detachments in battle gear arrived to take up positions around the ghetto. The diesel exhaust of the heavy trucks left dark brown trails of foul-smelling vapors behind, making it difficult to breathe. Small groups of SS officers dressed in their best and displaying rows of ribbons and other Nazi paraphernalia on their chests congregated at intersections outside the ghetto. They talked excitedly, passing bottles of French liqueur to one another.

As Reiner and his trio approached the last manned intersection outside the main gate of the ghetto a group of SS officers stopped them. Reiner quickly pulled a letter from his leather pouch, unfolded it, and held it up for inspection. The officers examined it, asked some questions, and, returning Reiner's Nazi salute, told him to proceed.

As they passed a church a small wedding party with a priest was coming out. A young photographer was taking pictures. The Orensteins heard the young bride say aloud, "I wonder where he's taking them," but no one answered. Two German soldiers came out of a building and, noticing the trio under escort, stopped for a few seconds, smiling knowingly.

Moving along Żeromskiego Street, the little party soon arrived at a building marked #25, which they entered through the gate. Two little boys raced tricycles at the far end of the yard. Another fifty meters to the right was a double door leading to the photographic studio that had belonged to the Orensteins, and which was now the property of the Nazis. Reiner fished a key from his pants pocket, opened the padlock, and, entering after the Orensteins, locked the door from the inside.

"Thank God we're here," he said in his heavy Viennese dialect, taking off his helmet. Orenstein's wife, hugging the boy with tears in her eyes, thanked him profusely for his deed. "I'll never forget what you did for us, Herr Reiner," she vowed, touching the sleeve of his tunic. He just looked at her and smiled.

"Now that we're here I might as well tell you about the letter. The signature on that letter that I showed to the SS at the intersection is a fake, and we were very lucky. I'm going to leave you here for the next two days," Reiner said. "You must be absolutely quiet and not let anybody in, no matter who they are. I'm taking the key with me. By Tuesday, I think, everything will be over, and I'll be back. I must get back to my station; God only knows what is awaiting me there. I beg you not to worry. The worst is over, so relax now. Let me have some water, please, and I shall take my leave."

Mrs. Orenstein went to the back of the studio and brought a tall glass of water for Reiner. He emptied it with two long gulps and wiped his mouth with the back of his hand. "By the

70

way," he said, "I left some food for you in the closet. Nothing fancy, but it should suffice."

"We thank you wholeheartedly, Herr Reiner," Mr. Orenstein said.

"Well, then, good-bye until Tuesday," Reiner replied, and he left. He locked the double gate from the outside and pinned on it a sizable white sign that read "Confiscated by order of the Gestapo."

Reiner was the photographer at the Gestapo headquarters, and Orenstein, a master in his art, was his negative retoucher. High-ranking Gestapo officials were not to be photographed in privately owned studios; photography at Gestapo headquarters became solely Reiner's responsibility.

As soon as Reiner had heard about the upcoming deportation in the ghetto he decided to keep Orenstein out of it. He had known him for over a year; he respected him for his superb craftsmanship and punctuality. Reiner knew that he was taking a chance protecting a Jew, but he was willing to do it; it wasn't in his nature to turn his back on people in need of help, particularly on an esteemed friend. The whole idea smelled of danger, but it could have been more dangerous to be shipped to the Russian front.

He certainly didn't want to fight the Russians. Reiner knew that the Nazis had no chance against them; Napoleon and others before him had tried and failed. The country was immense, the winters were severe, and partisans were everywhere, he was told. As far as he was concerned, he had had enough fighting. When in Vienna on furlough he had even told his wife what a decent couple the Orensteins were and how badly off the Polish Jews were; she had approved of his helping them.

Reiner wanted to stay in Poland as long as he possibly could. Things weren't too bad for him there. If he could only have Orenstein, his photography operation at the Gestapo might be assured, and he might not have to go to the east. He contemplated taking it up with his superior, Obersturmführer

Rauscht, but decided against it. He felt that Rauscht wouldn't like the idea, especially since it involved a Jew. That was when he decided to take the responsibility upon himself.

"Just in case the tide turns. After all, this war won't go on forever. One must look further than one's own nose," he had told his wife, Trude.

After Reiner left the studio the Orensteins collapsed from near exhaustion. Their anxieties had nearly paralyzed them, especially after they had learned that the signature on the letter was a fake. If it was discovered, it could mean their lives; the thought made them even more nervous.

Orenstein's wife stretched out a blanket on the studio floor and put the boy down. He promptly fell asleep. It was time for him to eat, but he couldn't tolerate food. He was losing strength by the hour, and his parents knew that there was little hope for him. Only a miracle could save him. Quietly they sat back, staring at his little face and listening to his irregular breathing.

They heard noises from the outside; every time someone walked near the doorway their hearts would stop. They only hoped that no one had seen them coming into the studio. In the worst case they could escape by the back door, but where would they go with a sick child? Who would take them in?

They sat on the floor with their backs against the wall, conversing in a whisper. Even whispering seemed loud to them, however; they remembered seeing a Nazi poster outside the gate calling on all Germans to be silent. "The enemy is listening," the poster boasted in big, bold letters.

Their mutual desperation seemed to have brought the Orensteins closer. "At least," Mrs. Orenstein kept saying, "we are together as a family. Whatever the outcome, we must be determined to stay together." Her husband listened and, sighing heavily, shook his head in agreement. There wasn't much for him to say. He knew how helpless they were, and his helpnessness only added to his anger.

The couple sat there whispering to each other late into the

night when suddenly a deafening racket of rifle fire rang out, followed by loud roars of speeding vehicles. They knew that the deportation in the ghetto had begun. They feared that Reiner might show up at any minute to deliver them back to the ghetto; perhaps the rescue had been an artificial gesture on the Austrian's part. As much as they were in his debt, they still had reason to distrust him. After all, he was a member of the Gestapo.

The shooting continued throughout the night, and the boy kept twisting and turning, calling out to his parents from his disturbed sleep. The Orensteins worried about the family and friends they had left behind in the ghetto. Would they all be deported? Would anyone be left? Perhaps it would have been better to have gone with them.

It was dawn when the shooting subsided. Orenstein walked to the door and noticed a thin streak of daylight stealing through the narrow crack of the double gate. He stretched out on the floor and promptly fell asleep, the light touching his shoulder. This was as close as he came to the outside world that day.

Another night set in for the Orensteins, and more rifle shots followed, only this time not as prolonged as the night before. When it was over there was complete silence. Not even footsteps could be heard; it was as if the world had come to an end.

When Reiner returned to his station that Sunday afternoon he found orders to report for duty. Shortly a truck sped him and his unit to the ghetto. They were to search apartments and cellars for anyone in hiding; the orders were to shoot on sight. Reiner found a woman with a child in her arms hiding in a cellar. He asked her to come out. He nearly begged her, but she refused. The frightened child stared at him with huge eyes and began crying. Reiner's superior officer was with him; he ordered Reiner to shoot. It made him sick, but he could not disobey the order. He fired.

After it was over he thought about the Orenstein boy. He

still couldn't understand why the woman had refused to come out of the cellar. It was suicidal, he thought. Being able to save the Orensteins made him feel better; it gave his bad conscience a sense of equilibrium. "There was nothing I could have done about the woman and child," he told his wife Trude when he saw her some months later. "They were going to die anyway."

After all, his was not a premeditated murder, Trude assured him. He was under orders, and in the long run he might have done the woman and child a favor by killing them instantly and preventing humiliation, torture, and ultimately death by gassing. They knew where these people were being shipped. Reiner had heard his superiors talk about it at headquarters some time before.

"Not a word to anybody, not even to your own wives," they had warned. It was a secret, and they were under oath, but most of the rank and file had found out, and some of them had even had a chance to witness it.

At first Trude had difficulty believing such stories, but she knew that Helmut told her the truth. "You must do what is right and just," she told him always.

Tuesday came, and the deportation was finished. Close to noon Reiner went to the studio. His expression had hardened, and he looked as if he needed sleep. He was abrupt, had little to say; he inquired how the Orensteins were and asked them to get ready. Now that the deportation was over he was going to escort them back to the new, smaller ghetto. "Going back won't be troublesome at all," he assured them.

The bright sunlight nearly blinded the Orensteins after almost three days in darkness, but the pleasant breeze felt invigorating. They were glad not to have to hide any longer; now they could speak to each other above a whisper. The boy smiled for the first time in days. He seemed to have lost weight, however, and he kept asking for water, unable to quench his thirst.

The new ghetto looked as though a storm had hit. There wasn't enough housing to accommodate the nearly five thousand people who remained; the little housing available was deplorable. With Reiner's intervention the Orensteins were given a room they would share with another couple and their two children. Their parents, their siblings, and most of their friends had been deported.

For almost another year Orenstein was employed by Reiner, retouching the Gestapo negatives. Occasionally Reiner would visit him in the ghetto, bringing along extra food.

Late in 1943 the last of the ghetto was liquidated, and the Orensteins were shipped to camps. The orders were to finalize the Jewish question, and there was nothing Reiner could do to save them. As far as he knew, there wasn't going to be a single Jew left in the whole of occupied Poland.

Meanwhile the Russian front kept advancing, and there was talk about his unit being shipped to the front lines. Happily, his diabetes started acting up; the Gestapo doctor ordered a medical leave, and Reiner went home to Vienna. Soon after he arrived the war came to an end.

The Orensteins survived the camps, although their son did not; soon after the deportation he died. After the war was over they found each other among the survivors searching for relatives all over the European continent. Sick and worn out, ridden with guilt and anger, they settled in Sweden.

After the war ended Reiner was troubled by nightmares. The woman and child he had shot in the ghetto in Radom kept appearing in his dreams. They disturbed him more and more, though only his wife Trude knew about his anxiety.

"Pull yourself together, Helmut," she counseled him. "Forget about all the bad things that happened. You must start a new life. You did all you could, and there is no reason for you to feel the way you do. You were under orders, and that was it."

Early one morning in the summer of 1945, standing in a breadline, Reiner was recognized by a former neighbor who denounced him as having belonged to the Gestapo. There were no other charges against him; only the Gestapo membership. Reiner was arrested.

Reiner's wife soon tired of the rumors she had to listen to every morning in the breadline. She wasn't the only one; everybody had a skeleton in his closet, and some of them were far larger than Reiner's, but it was nerve-racking all the same. She knew she should try to produce a statement from someone who had known Helmut during the occupation days in Poland. Trude couldn't think of anyone who had known him except the Orensteins, and they were probably dead. She didn't think they could have survived the camps; Helmut had told her what those places were like.

Still, she checked the camp survivor registers, published in papers and bulletins throughout Europe. Trude got hold of a newspaper that listed the Orensteins' address in Sweden. Hoping these were the right Orensteins, she quickly wrote them and told them what had happened to her husband. They were her only hope.

Before long she received an answer. Yes, they were the Orensteins she was looking for. They were happy to come to Vienna and do whatever was required of them; it was their chance to reciprocate.

"My dear Frau Reiner," Orenstein wrote, "Your husband saved us from deportation, risking his own life, and this we will never forget. You can count on us. We shall come to Vienna as soon as we get our travel permits."

Trude Reiner was touched by Orenstein's words. She was very eager to meet the couple; she hoped they would be her husband's saviors.

Within weeks the Orensteins arrived in Vienna. They brought along notarized testimony describing in detail Reiner's deeds on their behalf. Several days after the presentation of this testimony to the Allied Military Court Reiner was freed and cleared of his membership in the Gestapo and the Nazi party.

Naturally, Trude Reiner invited the Orensteins to join her family in a small celebration of Reiner's acquittal. "Just a few close relatives eager to meet you and raise a toast to Helmut's freedom," she told the Orensteins.

They gathered the following day at Reiner's apartment. There were several elderly women and a few men, mostly relatives, all dressed in their best. Reiner, in his loose-fitting suit (he had shed some weight in jail), embraced the Orensteins warmly and introduced them to those gathered.

"Now listen, everybody, I just want to say a few words," he announced in his deep, shaky voice. "I want you to meet my Jewish friends from Poland who turned out to be my saviors. I know it sounds strange, but it's true. Let's have a toast to the Orensteins; long live our friendship.

"But I want to say something else as well," he continued. "There is something that pains me a lot and disturbs my peace of mind. The eyes of a child follow me everywhere I go. . . . Maybe I shouldn't talk about it now, but it would be wrong not to. . . . Here I am celebrating my liberation, but my conscience will never be free. I don't think I can spell it out, but I would like you to know that terrible things were happening in Poland, and it pains me that I was a part of it, that I didn't do enough to stop it."

He started sobbing. His wife led him out of the room; a dead silence followed. The Orensteins couldn't understand the meaning of Reiner's speech and his reaction to his newfound freedom. Did he mean their little boy's eyes followed him? They would have liked to tell him again how much they appreciated what he had done for them and their son, but they were at a loss for words. Instead they sat at the table with total strangers, yesterday's enemies, now suddenly friends. It was all very confusing. Reiner's sudden breakdown further puzzled and dismayed them.

Trude Reiner returned to her guests. "I'm very sorry about what happened," she began, and, turning to the Orensteins, she continued, "I can't understand what upset him. He was in such high spirits and was so happy to hear that you survived the war. Perhaps the jail experience upset him. After all the things he has done for others, risking his own life, and then to be imprisoned—that must have been too much for him. Don't you think so?"

"Of course, we understand," Orenstein answered. "We have nothing but great respect and admiration for your husband, and we are ready to stand by him. That much we owe him."

There was nothing more the Orensteins could do in Vienna, where they felt uneasy and out of place; they planned to return to Sweden the following day. The war was over, and the Nazis were defeated; still, they felt surrounded by them, and they were uncomfortable.

"Why do you think Reiner risked his life to save us?" Orenstein asked his wife as soon as they were back at their hotel room that evening. "I can't believe he could have done it for selfish reasons. One really has to be decent and courageous at heart, don't you think?"

After a moment Mrs. Orenstein answered, "Whatever his reason was, were the roles reversed, I still wonder if any of us could equal him in his deed. The only thing that puzzles me is his speech; I still don't know whose eyes follow him and why. But I have no right to ask. That's his business."

The Orensteins sat up most of the night reminiscing about their time in hiding in the dark studio, only three years earlier; it seemed much further away somehow. They continued to wonder about the fates of their deported relatives and friends, whom they still felt they had betrayed.

"There are no words to express the guilt," Mrs. Orenstein said after some discussion, and she began to cry. Her husband comforted her and urged her to sleep.

It was still early when the telephone woke them. Trude Reiner asked them to stay on in Vienna. A terrible tragedy had taken place, she told them. Helmut was dead. He had accidentally shot himself that morning while dismantling a gun.

THE LAST MORNING

I very clearly remember the day I saw my mother for the last time. It was Sunday the sixteenth of August, 1942, a beautiful day with a clear blue sky and hardly a breeze. That morning she got up very early, earlier than usual, and quietly, so as not to wake us, she went out to the garden. I was already up. I watched her through the kitchen window. She sat down on the broken bench behind the lilac tree and cried. I always felt bad when I saw my mother cry, and this time it was even more painful.

My mother was going to be forty-four years old at the end of August. She never made a fuss over her birthday, as if it were her own secret, and so I never knew the exact date. She was of medium height, rather plump, with a most beautiful face. She had large brown eyes and long, dark brown hair sprinkled with gray, which she pulled back into a chignon. She smiled at people when she spoke and looked them straight in the eye.

When she came in from the garden she walked over to me and caressed my face as she used to do some years before the war, when I was a little boy. Now I was in my teens. Then she went over to the kitchen stove and started a fire. The wood was damp, and the kitchen filled with smoke. There was no more firewood left; this was the last of the broken-down fence from around our garden. She stood next to the stove fanning the smoke and asked me to open the door and the windows to let the smoke escape. Her eyes were red and teary, but when she turned to face me she smiled.

Soon the rest of the family was up, and Mother served a chicory brew with leftovers of sweet bread she had managed to bake some days earlier. There was even some margarine and jam, a great treat. We sat wherever we could, since the table was too small for the five of us. Because of limited table space my grandmother and my aunt ate their meals in their own room. None of us had much to say that morning. We just stared at one another as if to reaffirm our presence.

Suddenly my mother lifted her eyes and, looking at my father, asked him, "What are you thinking about?" My father, as if he had just wakened from a deep sleep, answered, "I stopped thinking, it's better not to think." We looked at him oddly. How could anyone stop thinking?

My mother got up from the table and started to tidy up the room. Then she asked me to go up to the attic and find her small brown suitcase for her. I found the suitcase, and, alone in the attic, I hugged it many times before I brought it to her.

The tension in the house nearly paralyzed me. It was stifling. I left in a hurry and, running all the way, went to investigate the ghetto square. It was still early in the morning, and clusters of people were congregating at street corners, pointing up at the utility poles. During the night the light bulbs had been replaced by huge reflectors. The ghetto police were out in force, preventing people from gathering. I noticed a poster reminding all inhabitants of the ghetto to deliver every sick or infirm member of their families to the only ghetto hospital. Noncompliance called for the death penalty.

My paternal grandmother was recovering from a stroke. She was able to walk with the help of a cane. I trembled at the thought of having to turn her in. The Nazis were preparing something devious. I knew the hospital wasn't big enough to absorb all the sick people in the ghetto.

My mother studied my face when I came back from the square. There was a frightened look in her eyes. She asked me what was happening out there, what people were saying, and I lied to her. I didn't mention the reflector bulbs, but I could tell that she knew what was coming.

She had her suitcase packed, and her neatly folded raincoat was laid out on the couch, as if she were going on an overnight trip the way she used to before the war. No one said much. We were communicating through our silence; our hearts were tense. My father took out the old family album and stood at the window, slowly turning the heavy pages. I looked over his shoulder and saw him examining his own wedding picture. He pulled it out of the album and put it inside his breast pocket. I pretended not to see.

My mother started preparing our lunch, and I helped her with the firewood. There was no more fence left, and somebody had just stolen our broken bench. I found an old tabletop that Father kept behind the house, covered with sheets of tar paper. It was dry and burned well. I didn't tell my mother where the wood had come from; I was afraid she might not like the idea of putting a good table to the fire.

It was past noon, and my mother was busy in the kitchen. She found some flour and potatoes she had managed to save and came up with a delicious soup, as well as potato pancakes sprinkled with fried onions. Was this to be our last meal together? I wondered.

Some friends and neighbors with scared expressions on their faces dropped in to confirm the rumors about the coming deportation and to say good-bye. The Zilber family came, and everybody cried. I couldn't bring myself to say good-bye to anybody; I feared that I would never see them again.

It was getting close to four o'clock in the afternoon when my grandmother, dressed in her best, came out of her room. She was ready, she said, if someone would escort her to the hospital. My brother and I volunteered. She insisted on walking alone, so we held her lightly by the arms in case she tripped. She walked erect, head high; from time to time she would look at one of us without saying a word. People passed us in bewilderment. They seemed like caged birds looking for an escape. An elderly man carrying a huge bundle on his shoulders stopped us and asked for the time. "Why do you need to know the time?" I inquired. He looked at me as if upset by my question and answered, "Soon it will be time for evening prayers, don't you know?" And he went on his way, talking to himself and balancing the awkward bundle on his shoulders.

When we reached the hospital gate my grandmother insisted we leave her there. She would continue alone. With a heavy heart I kissed her good-bye. She smiled and turned toward us, saying, "What does one say? Be well?" Then she disappeared behind the crumbling whitewashed gate of the hospital. I needed to cry but was ashamed to do so in front of my older brother. Determined to prove how tough I was, I held back my tears. We walked back in silence, each of us probably thinking the same thing.

I'll never forget coming back to the house after escorting Grandmother to the hospital. My mother was in the kitchen saying good-bye to one of her friends. I had never seen her cry as she was crying. When she saw us she fell upon us, and through her tears she begged us to go into hiding. She begged us to stay alive so that we could tell the world what had happened. Her friend was crying with her, and I felt my heart escaping.

A neighbor came in to tell us that the ghetto was surrounded by armed SS men, and it was official that the deportation was about to begin. The ghetto police were on full alert, and it was impossible to get any information out of them.

My brother and I turned and ran out of the house. Without stopping we ran the entire length of the ghetto until, dripping with sweat, we arrived at the fence. On the other side of the fence was a Nazi officers' club; farther off in the middle of a field stood a stable. By now the Ukrainian guards with their rifles were inside the ghetto. We scaled the fence behind their backs and made it across to the other side. We entered the stable through a side door. As far as I could tell, no one was there. The horses turned their heads and sized us up. My brother decided we should hide separately, so that if one of us was discovered, the other one would still have a chance. I climbed up on the rafters and onto a wooden platform wedged in between two massive beams. There was enough hay to cover myself with, and I stretched out on my stomach. Through the wide cracks between the boards of the platform I could scan the entire stable underneath me. I also found a crack in the wall that allowed me a wide view of the street across from the stable.

A mouse came out from under a pile of straw, stopped for a second, and ran back in. I lay there trying to make sense of every sound. As I turned on my side I felt something bulky inside my pocket. I reached for it and discovered a sandwich wrapped in brown paper. My mother must have put it there when my jacket was still hanging behind the kitchen door.

As I replaced the sandwich I heard the door open and saw a man enter. He walked to the other end of the stable and deposited a small parcel inside a crate. Then he started to tend to the horses while whistling an old Polish tune. He must be the caretaker, I thought. He appeared to be still young, even though I couldn't clearly see his face; he walked briskly and carried heavy bales of hay with ease. I feared the commotion he was causing might attract attention; he kept going in and out, filling the water bucket for the horses to drink. I was getting hungry. I was about to bite into the sandwich when on one of his trips he looked up at the spot where I was hiding. I froze. Could it be that he had heard me move? I couldn't imagine what had made him look up, and I broke out in a sweat. I held on to the sandwich but was too upset to eat it. Every time he opened the door it squeaked, and the spring attached to it caused it to shut with a loud bang. He spoke to the horses in Polish with a provincial accent and called each horse by its name. He lingered with some of them, slapped their backs or gently patted their necks. How I envied him. Why was he free while I had to hide?

I started to recall the events of the entire day. I realized I had run out of the house without saying good-bye to my parents. Seized with guilt, I started sobbing.

I must have fallen asleep. When I woke up I heard loud noises coming from behind the fence. I looked through the crack in the wall; it was dark outside. Suddenly a loud chorus of cries and screams rang out, intermingled with voices shouting commands in German. Rifle shots followed, and more voices calling out names pierced the darkness. The cries of little children made me shudder.

I imagined hearing the screaming of my four-year-old cousin, who was there with his mother; my aunt, her sister, with her two beautiful little daughters. They were all there, trapped, desperate, and helpless. I thought of our friend Mr. Gutman, who some years before had claimed that God was in exile. I wondered where he was and what he was saying now. I worried about my grandmother and what they were doing to her at the hospital. Frightened and burdened with my misgivings, I resolved to go on, not to give in.

I heard the squeak of the door and looked down to see the caretaker slipping out. He blocked the door with a rock to keep it open. The sounds coming in from the outside were getting louder; the horses became restless and started to neigh. Rifle shots were becoming more frequent and sounded much closer than before. All these noises went on for most of the night—it felt like an eternity.

I could picture my mother in that screaming, weeping crowd begging me to stay alive, and I could hear her crying for help. Was my father with her, I kept wondering, and where was my sister?

It was almost daybreak when the noises began to die down. The sun was rising; it looked like the beginning of a hot August day. Only occasional rifle shots could be heard, and a loud hum that sounded as if swarms of bees were flying overhead; it was the sound of thousands of feet shuffling against the pavement. Looking through the crack in the wall, I could see long columns of people being escorted by armed SS men with dogs on leashes. Most of the people carried knapsacks strapped to their backs; others carried in their arms what was left of their possessions. I focused on as many people as I could, hoping to recognize a face. I wanted to know if my mother was among them and kept straining my eyes until I couldn't see anymore. I wondered if my brother, at the other end of the stable, was able to see outside. As it was, we had no way to communicate.

I kept imagining the moving columns of people getting longer and wider until there was no more room for them to walk. As I pictured them they kept multiplying; soon they walked over one another like ants in huge anthills, and the SS men weren't able to control them any longer.

Suddenly I heard voices underneath me. Before I realized who was there I saw the caretaker climbing up toward my hiding place. I couldn't believe it. I stopped breathing. Two SS men wearing steel helmets and carrying rifles stood at the door watching the caretaker climb. He came close to the platform where I was lying and in a loud voice told me to get down. "They came to get you," he said. "I knew you were here hiding. You can't outsmart me." I was betrayed.

Next he walked right over to where my brother was hiding and called him out. The two of us took a terrible beating from the SS men before they escorted us back to the ghetto. The first thing I saw in the ghetto was a large horse-drawn cart on rubber wheels, loaded with dead, naked bodies. On one side, pressed against the boards, was my grandmother. She seemed to be looking straight at me.

No dictionary in the world could supply the words for what I saw next. My mother begged me to be a witness, however; all these years I've been talking and telling, and I'm not sure if anybody listens or understands me. I myself am not sure if I understand.

The following night my brother and I miraculously escaped the final deportation, only to be shipped off to the camps separately soon afterward. I never saw my mother again, nor was I ever able to find a picture of her. Whenever I want to remember her I close my eyes and think of that Sunday in August of 1942 when I saw her sitting in our ghetto garden, crying behind the lilac tree.

ANTON THE DOVE FANCIER

Directly across from the apartment building in which I used to live stood a long row of attached wooden sheds. It was easy enough to climb up on the roof from where the garbage bin stood and run along the entire length to the sheds, to where a pear tree grew out of the adjoining fruit orchard. By the middle of the summer the overhanging branches were heavy with clusters of ripe yellow pears; I would greedily fill my pockets with them. Mr. Rytman, the orchard owner, didn't like the idea at all, but as he was unable to climb onto the roof, he was relatively powerless. I can still remember him shaking his fist at me from below, his face red with anger.

When the weather was good I could stretch out on my back at the edge of the roof and watch Anton train his pigeons in the adjoining yard. The sky above me would fill with them, many of them white, others brown or gray, spotted with blue or purple, sporting fancy broad tails, their colors splendidly reflecting in the sunlight. They would dart about or hide behind puffy clouds or aim for the sun, flying higher and higher, constantly changing course and finally dissolving into tiny, moving specks.

Anton, waving a long pole with a scrap of red cloth attached to it, would whistle shrilly. The pigeons seemed to respond to his commands; often even strays would join his flock and land on top of his dovecote. He would throw fits and go into endless tirades of cursing when one of his pigeons got lost. From the way he raged at the sky, it seemed as though he were screaming at God himself.

A husky, well-built man, probably in his thirties, Anton was the janitor in the building next to ours. He had a broad, ruddy face with high cheekbones and light blue eyes set far apart. When he spoke several gold teeth glistened. In warm weather he wore striped polo shirts; on Sundays he dressed in white and looked to me like the neighborhood ice cream vendor. At all times a silver chain with a sizable crucifix dangled outside his shirt.

When his pigeons weren't flying Anton would stretch out under the linden trees and sleep. Nothing could wake him, not even bands of fighting, screaming children in the middle of a game of hide-and-seek. When his wife needed him she just shook him by his shoulders and pulled him to his feet. She was a blond, big-chested woman, almost as tall as Anton himself. As soon as he woke up he would mumble, "What happened? I'm coming right away."

"Look at me, you drunken swine," she would yell, holding on to him. "I'm not your prize white pigeon, I'm your wife. Can you recognize me? Now get up and come with me. There is trouble with the plumbing."

Anton's wife was perpetually cleaning, performing most of the janitor's chores, in fact. One could see her early in the morning sweeping the sidewalk or washing the windows. Anton hardly ever lent a hand; he was too busy raising pigeons and scolding his wife whenever he could find an excuse to do so. If anything went wrong in the building, the tenants would call on her. To them she was Mrs. Anton, as if she didn't have a name of her own.

Anton was a moody man, even with the pigeons. Sometimes he treated them as if they were people; other times he would threaten to have them cooked. Sometimes he would show up at the dovecote with a bottle of vodka sticking out of his back pocket. He would let out the pigeons and—holding onto the long pole with one hand—manage to fish his vodka out with the other. His face would turn red, and then he would scream his favorite line to his pigeons: "Fly, fly, my beautiful birds, but do come back again." As soon as the pigeons landed Anton would stretch out on the grass; in a drunken voice, slurring the lyrics, he would sing old Polish patriotic songs.

Anton's ambition was to lure away prize males from other breeders by launching his prize females. He considered his a gentleman's sport but saw nothing wrong with kidnapping other dove fanciers' birds. The competition was enormous, and some pigeons had high price tags on them, he once told me. Anton preferred the pure white ones to all other pigeons; they were the smartest, he claimed, and he was ready to give away a liter of vodka to anybody who could lure away one of his pure white birds. "The secret behind it is to feed them well and give them lots of freedom," he would remind me. "The more you fly them, the more they want to come back. They know what is waiting for them. They're intelligent birds."

Generally Anton would fly his pigeons only when the weather was good. At other times he cleaned the dovecote or made repairs around the building. During the winters, when the dovecote got snowed in, one could hear the cooing of his cooped-up, restless birds trying to get out. Anton had insulated the dovecote on the outside with straw mats; he cleaned the inside every day. He took it badly when one of his pigeons got sick or died.

One Sunday morning in the spring of 1939 I watched Anton participate in a competition. At a set time all the dove fanciers in the area let their pigeons out; the person who succeeded in luring the other breeders' pigeons would get to keep them. This was the only occasion on which kidnapped pigeons became the property of the winner.

The sun was out, and the sky was full of drifting white

clouds. Soon several flocks of pigeons appeared in the sky. They came from every direction, flying in formations and breaking up into smaller groups, hiding behind the clouds. They joined ranks and broke away and flew around in circles. At one point a huge mass of pigeons covered the entire neighborhood sky, nearly blocking out the sun.

Anton became frantic when his pigeons flew out of sight. He cursed and whistled no end; I had never heard such words before. Some tenants whose apartments faced the sheds closed their windows. Small flocks of frightened sparrows and starlings took off from nearby roofs and branches, scared off by Anton's swearing and whistling. Even the neighborhood's stray cats fled.

Soon the pigeons reappeared in three separate formations. They circled lower and lower; finally one group broke away and landed on top of Anton's dovecote. Anton stood nearby, trap wire in hand, ready to let go as soon as the pigeons landed. I was on the roof watching. When he noticed me he yelled, "Did you see what my birds brought me? Three prize pigeons. I saw them land with my own eyes!" I couldn't understand how anybody could tell one pigeon from another; at close range Anton, it seemed, could recognize his pigeons even in flight.

At the end of that summer, after the war had broken out and the Nazis had occupied the city, I lost track of Anton. Occasionally when leaving the house in the morning I would see his pigeons in flight; occasionally I would hear him carry on behind the sheds.

One cold morning in the middle of the winter of 1940–41, on my way to work, I saw Anton in handcuffs being escorted by two Gestapo men dressed in black leather coats. They pushed him into a dark green van and took off with him at high speed. Soon I found out why: The Nazis had requisitioned Anton's pigeons, and when they came to get them they found them all dead inside the dovecote. Anton was arrested by the Gestapo and charged with sabotage of the German Reich.

Some months passed, and nobody in the building, including his wife, had any news of Anton. There were rumors that he had become a pigeon trainer for the German army and that he was well off, living somewhere in Germany. His wife continued to take care of the building—one could see her in the early morning sweeping the sidewalk—but I didn't dare ask her about Anton. I felt bad about his arrest and couldn't imagine how he could live without his pigeons. One day I saw his wife breaking apart the dovecote and chopping it up for firewood. The trap wire got thrown into a corner next to the fence; the long pole with the red cloth disappeared.

After Anton's arrest most of the dove fanciers in the neighborhood lost interest in raising pigeons. If their pigeons weren't confiscated by the Nazis, they got rid of them in different ways. Once in a while I could see a stray cruising over the yard.

Late in 1943, when the Nazis liquidated the last of our ghetto, I was apprehended and shipped to the Maidanek death camp. Coming out of the showers just after my arrival, I noticed a man who looked like Anton; he was dressed like a *kapo.* He threw a pair of wooden clogs and torn socks at me. I had to keep running to catch the pieces of clothing that were being thrown in my direction; there was no time to stop and look back. Outside, in the middle of a snowy field, still dripping wet from the shower, I managed to get dressed. The pants and jacket were sizes too large, and the sleeveless shirt, hopelessly too small, had no buttons. The clogs and an outlandish World War I military cap completed my costume; I had no overcoat.

While trying to pull on the torn socks I saw someone walking in my direction. He was tall and wore a striped prisoner's uniform and shiny black leather boots; his neck was wrapped with an orange scarf. It was indisputably Anton. I was astounded. He stopped and said, "You're the kid from Radom, aren't you? You used to sit on the roof and watch me fly my pigeons, right?" I was speechless and could only shake my head yes. "How did they get you? This is no place for you, my boy," he advised, and he walked away.

Not in my wildest dreams had I expected to meet Anton in Maidanek. But there wasn't much time to think about it; several SS guards soon appeared with German shepherds on leashes. Screaming, cursing, and swinging their heavy sticks, they urged the new arrivals over an icy field to an area filled with rows of long wooden barracks surrounded by double barbed-wire fences. Every hundred meters or so was a watchtower with a mounted machine gun pointing down at us; steel-helmeted guards dressed in sheepskin stood behind the guns, watching. A tall brick chimney loomed in the background, dominating the entire landscape. A thin veil of smoke was rising from it; a very unusual stench, a little like burned chicken feathers, permeated the entire field.

The frozen ground was covered with a thick sheet of ice. It was impossible to walk in clogs without slipping or falling, so I took mine off and ran in my stocking feet. Finally, after several hours of standing in formation, we were rushed inside the barracks. Starved, numb, and frozen to the bone, I tasted my first bowl of a dark-brown liquid resembling coffee. It was the famous Nazi ersatz—substitute. Whatever it was, it thawed me out; I could feel its warmth travel to the tips of my fingers. It was miraculous, I thought, to be alive.

I couldn't get Anton off my mind as I tried to concentrate on my new environment. I was to share a bunk with someone my age whom I had met in the transport. The straw sack was nearly empty, and the torn scraps of a leftover blanket weren't big enough to cover one of our frozen bodies. We lay in our stiff clothing, shaking from the cold, afraid to breathe, and spent the night huddled close together. My bunk mate was silent. When he spoke it was in a faint, shaky whisper. He mourned the loss of his parents and his little brother during the last deportation. Hushed voices could be heard all night long. Someone cried out. Others called out their mother's or their wife's names. Every now and then a voice could be heard reciting a prayer for the dead, or beseeching God. I don't remember ever falling asleep that night. Before I knew it the lights went on; although it was still dark outside, it was time to get up. I wondered how long one could endure such conditions.

The following Sunday Anton came to visit me. He carried a bundle under his arm. "I brought you some warm things to wear," he said, handing me the entire bundle.

"Thank you so much, but I don't have anything to pay you with," I blurted out, extending my hand to shake his.

"Don't be a fool. Did I ask you for payments? I'm in a position to help you, so take it. Maybe one day you will have to help me. Who knows? Everything is possible in this crazy, screwed-up world." He pulled out a large chunk of bread, stuck it inside my pocket, and said, "Eat the bread. Don't let them steal it from you." He turned and walked briskly out of the barrack. People standing near the door stepped aside to clear a path for him. There was fear in their eyes.

I walked back to my bunk and opened the bundle. I found a thick lined jacket, a woolen scarf, and a plaid flannel shirt. Inside the pockets of the jacket were two woolen socks. I was touched by Anton's generosity, though I couldn't understand why he was going out of his way for me. I told my bunk mate about Anton and that evening shared the extra bread with him that Anton had given me. At night we covered ourselves with the heavy jacket; for the first time since my arrival I was able to sleep.

The following night, as I was covering myself, I felt a small bulge in the jacket's lining. I ripped it open just wide enough to put two fingers inside, and when no one was looking I fished out a stiff, folded piece of brown paper. Inside it was a coin. I decided not to tell anybody, not even my bunk mate. After all, the jacket had come from Anton. Shouldn't I tell him? Shouldn't he know what was hidden in it? Alone in the latrine I managed to read the engraved inscription. It was an American ten-dollar gold coin. I knew that one could get the death penalty for hiding foreign currency; I put the coin back inside the brown paper and stuck it inside my sock. The following day my bunk mate was transferred to another barrack, and there was no one around I could trust or ask for advice. I decided to tell Anton about the coin when I saw him. How else could I express my gratitude for all the things he had done for me?

Some days later Anton showed up. He brought some food and two aspirins, in case I got a cold. We moved to the other side of the barracks, where there were fewer people. When I told him about my find he looked at me in disbelief.

"You're stupid," he said. "Why did you tell me? You could have had a real party with ten dollars. I never knew that there was a coin behind the lining. If I did, you would never have seen it, I can assure you. Ten dollars could buy you a kilo of ham, two loaves of white bread, and a kilo of sugar. Real sugar, not saccharin."

"I would rather you take it," I answered. "It's yours." I retrieved the piece of folded paper and inconspicuously handed it over to him. He took it from me in the same manner and kept it in his hand. I noticed some people watching us, but Anton didn't pay much attention. He was a powerful *kapo,* and nobody except the SS could challenge him. I was glad to have gotten rid of the coin and didn't want to risk my life over it. I tried not to think of all the ham and bread I could have bought with it.

That night I dreamt about Anton. He was swinging a huge pink ham on a rope, and every time I tried to reach for it, it would bounce back before I had a chance to raise my arm. That morning I got up hungry and more frustrated than ever. I still couldn't understand how one could purchase hams and other food items in a camp. Even outside, such things were difficult to find.

Some weeks went by, and soon winter drew to an end. The snow began to melt; the air got warmer. There were rumors that the war on the Russian front was getting closer, and in fact, thunderlike rumblings of heavy artillery could be heard at night. Before long the Nazis decided to evacuate the camp; everyone in our barracks was told to get ready for transport.

The following morning, as I was about to board the truck, Anton showed up. He brought an aluminum flask full of water, stuffed my pockets with extra bread, and gave me a pack of cigarettes.

"I don't have to teach you any longer what you must do," he said, "but if you want to stay alive, you'll know. Don't smoke, but trade the cigarettes for food. Cigarettes are better than gold. One more thing. If you happen to see my wife before I do, tell her that I'm fine."

I was still shaking his hand when the trucks started their engines. Anton put his hands on my shoulders, and tears welled up in his eyes. Over the roar of the diesel engines I heard him say, "Don't let them get you." We climbed into the trucks. Then we were on a cattle train heading south. Nobody knew where. The water Anton gave me kept me going for the entire trip. Every drop I took reminded me of his generosity.

Some months and two camps later, in August of 1944, I arrived in Mauthausen, Austria, where for three weeks I walked up and down 112 steps six times daily to carry rock out of a stone quarry on my bare shoulders. A man I met in the soup line whom I remembered from Maidanek began a conversation. "Did you know that your friend *kapo* Anton got his treatment in the last transport out of Maidanek?" he asked me. "He got what was coming to him. They say he didn't hesitate to kill a man for the slightest infraction, or to help a man he liked. He was a strong and moody bastard. I also heard that they found on him a lot of foreign currency and jewelry. People were wondering how he had gotten it."

He wanted to know if I was interested in trading some soup for a silk scarf. He pulled out of his pocket a small, creased, bloodstained orange cloth. "It looks like the same one Anton used to wear around his neck," I remarked. One had to be a *kapo* to parade around a concentration camp with a silk scarf, and Anton was the only one in my experience who dared.

"It's silk," he said. "Wouldn't you want to have it?"

"Where did you get it?" I asked him.

"I was in the last transport out of Maidanek," he started telling me, "and some people in our car roughed up some *kapos* and stripped them of their clothing. Anton was among them. When we arrived in Mauthausen I found the scarf on the floor of the car."

"Did they kill Anton?" I asked. My companion seemed surprised at such naïveté.

"What do you think?" he answered, placing the scarf in the palm of my hand. "I don't want any soup. You can keep it," he said, walking back toward the barracks.

In April the first signs of spring arrived; early in May the SS hierarchy disappeared, and only the low-ranking Ukrainian and Lithuanian guards remained. They installed a tall mast on the camp grounds and hoisted the Red Cross flag. We didn't go to work anymore, and our food rations were finished. Typhoid and dysentery were rampant, and very few of us were able to walk. One early afternoon, on May 5, 1945, three American reconnaissance tanks lost their way to Linz and by chance came across our camp. We were free.

Some months later I went back to Radom to look for my relatives. The day I arrived, as I was walking down the street in my old neighborhood, I met Anton's wife. I introduced myself and told her I had met Anton in Maidanek.

"I already know what happened to Anton," she volunteered. "His own people killed him. I also know who you are. I remember you. You used to live in the building next to ours," she continued. "Could you come by later in the afternoon to see me?" she asked. "I would like you to read some letters for me. The woman who used to read for me has moved away, and there is no one in the building I can trust," she said.

"How can you trust me?" I asked. "You hardly know me." Anton's wife looked straight into my eyes and smiled knowingly.

ANTON THE DOVE FANCIER

Late in the afternoon I arrived at her apartment. It was a large room filled with lots of furniture. Over the bed hung a framed picture of her with her husband; above that hung a crucifix. Anton's wife went to the dresser and pulled out two letters. Both had been written by Anton when he was in Maidanek. One had the seal of the Nazi censor; the other one, she said, was sent to her by a Polish underground contact. They were written in pencil, faintly, and with many misspellings. One paragraph especially was of interest to me.

It read: "Do you remember that skinny Jewish kid next door who used to watch me fly the pigeons before the war? Well, he is here with me now. You know how much I always disliked these people, God forgive me, but when I saw him running out of the showers, naked, in the middle of winter, something told me that I should help him. I felt sorry for him, even though he isn't one of us."

I never read that passage aloud to Anton's wife, but I read her the rest of the letter. I told her how difficult it was to decipher his handwriting. And I told her how much Anton had helped me in the camp and what a generous man he was. She looked at me in disbelief.

"To me he wasn't generous at all," she said, moving closer. Her breath smelled of alcohol. "He was more generous to his pigeons.

"I had a very tough life with Anton," she continued. "God forgive me for saying it, but it's the truth. He only loved his pigeons. That was all he lived for.

"You must be hungry," she said, moving toward the cupboard. She came back carrying a bottle of vodka and two small glasses, which she placed in the center of the table. Then she prepared a plate of tiny sandwiches. "There is much to celebrate," she said, setting down the plate and pouring the vodka into the two glasses.

I disliked vodka, but I was embarrassed to admit as much, and so I picked up the glass. With one motion I poured the liquid into my mouth. It burned my throat, but after the second glass it began to go down smoothly. My eyes teared, and my head began to feel heavy. It felt as if a fire were burning inside me.

Anton's wife sat across the table staring right through me. "Call me Nela," she said, breathing heavily. "I'm now going to tell you something that you probably won't believe. I was born into the Jewish faith. When I was a child my parents died; an aunt took me in, but she was poor, she had a sick husband, and she couldn't really take care of me. When I was in my teens I ran away. Then I met a Polish woman who took an interest in me and was good to me. She was Anton's mother. She ran a whorehouse. Before long she made me work for her. I was only fifteen then. Some months after that I met Anton, and he fell in love with me. He took me away from his mother and brought me here. We were never married, because I didn't have a birth certificate; we just lived together. In the beginning he didn't know that I was a Jewess, and I was afraid to tell him. Sometimes he suspected, but he was never sure. The fact that I was blond and blue-eyed confused him, and I spoke Polish better than he ever did.

"What bothered me most was when he got drunk and angry. He would insult me and sometimes even hit me, but I fought back. He was very lazy and couldn't do a thing for himself, but I knew how to make him comfortable. I wanted to have a child, but for some reason it didn't work out. I suspected that Anton wanted to have children, and that was why he started raising pigeons. They were his babies. If I had had any relatives, I would have left him, but I had no place to go, not even a friend, so I decided to wait. Now that he's gone I won't stay here much longer. I'll probably try to go to Palestine. They say that Jews can go there now. I want to be among my own people. I'm still young, and I hope to be able to find a good man and get married. Don't you think I could? I still remember some Yiddish, even though I haven't used it since I was a child."

"I'm sure you will," I managed to say somehow; despite all that had happened, her story made me lose my sense of reality. It felt as if I was dreaming. Suddenly Anton's wife stood up and started to undress. She was tall and slender, and her long blond hair covered her pale shoulders. She took my hands and put them on her chest. "Don't be bashful," she said. "I'll show you."

She lifted me off the chair and pulled me toward the bed. I wasn't resisting; I was too weak and numb. It felt as if someone was massaging my back and my thighs. When I touched her face it was wet from tears. I wiped her face with the palm of my hand; she put her long, soft arms around me and gently pressed me against her bosom. That caress transcended every pleasurable moment I had ever known. For the first time in my life I felt secure.

"Will you stay with me for a while? Just for a while," she pleaded. "You could teach me how to read." I kept silent, afraid to make a sound, afraid that if I spoke, the comfort would dissolve. I could hear the raindrops hitting the windowpanes outside.

When I woke up the following morning Nela was gone. Her fluffy red cat sat at the foot of the bed, blinking, and when I looked up I saw Anton gazing down at me from the wall. I also heard voices outside arguing over a broken fence.

ON GUILT

A dim utility light from across the street shone through the curtainless window, outlining my father's dark, unshaven face. From my cot next to the window I could see his silhouetted figure against the wall. He spread his coat over an old, worn-out blanket he had found in an abandoned apartment. He kept turning and twisting most of the night, his body shaking as if in a spasm. I didn't think he ever slept. This went on every night, deep into the winter, the coldest I can remember. Curled up on a narrow iron bed, his head buried inside a soiled pillow, he would groan and whimper and sometimes break into a sob. Nights became unbearable; his groaning and crying out in his sleep got worse and worse.

I had never heard my father cry before. He was a tough and self-disciplined man, I thought, but since my mother had been taken away during the deportation he wasn't the same; he seemed to be lost without her.

All the same, he never mentioned Mother. Was it too painful for him to talk about? I wondered. And why had he let her go alone? The questions had nagged at me daily.

At times he would take out his own wedding picture and

look at it for the longest time. It was the only picture he had saved from the family album and the only thing he seemed to care about. He kept it in his breast pocket, neatly wrapped inside an old brown envelope, and never showed it to anybody. It was his personal property.

Then—as now—I had only a vague idea of what had taken place during the first night of the deportation; at my mother's insistence I had gone into hiding with my older brother Michael. My sister stayed behind with my parents. Only reluctantly and with much apprehension, some months after the deportation, did she tell me what she had seen.

"It was still early in the evening," she told me, "when the SS and the ghetto police stormed into the house, ordered us out, and chased us on the double to the square. In the beginning I was with our parents, but in all the confusion, with thousands of people running and pressing against one another, we got separated. When I finally arrived at the square I somehow managed to find them again.

"The loud chorus of the Nazis shouting commands was interrupted only by the frequent crackling of rifle shots; huge dogs were everywhere. It was impossible to distinguish one voice from another; mothers were calling for their children, children were crying and screaming for their parents.

"People were being shot at close range," she continued, "and tiny babies were being crushed with rifle butts or being thrown against brick walls by intoxicated SS men and Ukrainians. It was one big death orgy. They were killing for sheer pleasure. No one was there to stop them. The sound of glass breaking, people climbing over one another or tripping over their belongings, desperately trying to find their loved ones, and the frightening screams went on for most of the night.

"It must have been around midnight when Mother was taken away by a tall SS officer and put with the group to be deported," she continued, "but some minutes later she was brought back by another SS officer, a shorter one. After a sharp exchange between the two Nazis Mother was taken away again by the tall officer, who, this time, also tore up her papers. I tried to intervene, pointing out to him that Mother had all her necessary working papers, that she was a talented seamstress, that she was young, only in her early forties, and healthy.

"He refused to listen, slapped my face, and threatened to deport me, too, unless I shut up. There was nothing more I could have done," she recalled. "I couldn't have gone with Mother even if I had wanted to. This was the moment when I realized that Father was nowhere to be seen. I feared that he had already been deported. I was in a different group by now, separated from Mother, whose group was across the square, closely guarded by Ukrainians, armed SS men, and dogs.

"In desperation," my sister continued, "I raised my arm with a handkerchief as high as I could, hoping that Mother would notice me. I even called her name, but I don't imagine she could have heard me. I tried to shout good-bye to her, just to let her know that I was there. I wasn't sure any longer where she was, but I assumed that she was still in that group to be deported. People were screaming and shouting louder and louder, and there were bloodcurdling screams. It is difficult to describe what went on that night. If there is a Hell, I thought, this is probably what it looks like.

"When dawn came a strange calm prevailed. Littered with torn books, abandoned knapsacks, shoes, and clothing, the square looked like a battlefield. Here and there loaves of bread or half-eaten sandwiches could be seen in the gutters. Dead bodies were scattered all over the place, and a nauseating odor—like a mixture of rotten vegetables, human sweat, and urine—hung over the whole square. Window shutters swung in the morning breeze, squeaking and banging loudly against the walls of the deserted houses."

My sister fell silent, closed her eyes, and covered her face with her hands, then looked at me again. "I can still smell the whole rotten scene," she said quietly.

* * *

ON GUILT

Sometimes during that winter I could see my father talking to a stranger at a street corner or walking aimlessly by himself, looking at nothing in particular. He held his head low and kept his hands in his pockets, as if trying to hide something.

Occasionally, at the studio, I was able to buy some chocolate-filled wafers from my Polish black-market contact and to smuggle them into the ghetto for my father. One cold, snowy evening I saw him standing in a doorway displaying the chocolate wafers inside a cardboard box, trying to sell them. His hat was pulled over his eyes, his face wrapped inside a woolen scarf. That gray, miserable figure hawking chocolate wafers was my father. I realized how humiliating it would have been for him if he had seen me; I walked on quickly, hoping that he hadn't noticed me.

Some weeks went by, and spring was around the corner. One Sunday early in the morning my father asked me to go out with him.

"Let's go outside for a walk," he said quietly. "I would like to talk to you."

The ghetto was beginning to come alive as we went out into the narrow streets. It was a cold, crisp morning; the smell of freshly baked bread emanated from a bakery not far away. People were beginning to peek their frightened faces out of dark doorways and narrow passageways. First they stopped and looked to make sure it was safe. Somebody greeted my father, but he didn't hear. Lost in his thoughts, he kept walking, staring at the ground.

"I must tell you what happened during the night of the deportation," he suddenly began, "and how we lost Mother.

"You probably wonder why I didn't talk about it before," he said, almost in a whisper. "It's very painful for me to talk about it, but now the time has come for me to tell you. I hope you'll understand. Please listen.

"When the SS with the police chased us out of the house that evening they made us run all the way to the square. It was very difficult for Mother to run over the cobblestone streets, but she held on to me, and somehow we made it. On the way we lost all our belongings, and it bothered us that we had nothing left, not even a toothbrush. The only thing I was able to save were two sandwiches inside my coat pockets.

"Once in the square we were told to form lines; then they broke the lines, only to start forming them again. It was confusing and tiring. We couldn't stand on our feet any longer; it must have been past midnight when our line got moving and the Nazis finally started checking our working papers.

"When I turned for a second to get out my papers I realized suddenly that your mother and your sister weren't with me. The two of them were gone, as if they had evaporated. This was when the Nazis decided to separate men from women, but I wasn't aware of it. I remained in the same spot. I looked around, called their names over and over, but as hard as I tried, I couldn't find them. It took some time before I realized what had happened. I got very panicky, and I kept asking people around me for help, but nobody paid any attention. Everybody out there was looking for some relative of his own.

"I still didn't understand how all this could have happened. I was left alone," he said, looking down at me with bloodshot eyes.

"I never even had a chance to give your mother the sandwich I kept for her in my coat pocket. I forgot all about it. She had nothing left, not even her pocketbook."

He started crying; in a desperate gesture full of false hope I muttered, "Oh, I'm sure she's alive and we'll find her soon."

My father just looked at me with an expression full of disbelief and answered, "I hope you're right, I just hope so."

It was extremely difficult for me to watch him suffer. At that moment I wished he had gone with Mother. At least then they would be together.

I tried to keep up his spirits whenever I could and told him all kinds of lies and stories about Allied air raids and attempted landings on the French coast. I kept reassuring him that the war would be over soon, that the Nazis would be punished for their crimes, that Germany was in the process of being devastated by the Allied air forces.

As it turned out later, I had very nearly spoken the truth, though I didn't know it then. I based my accounts entirely on rumors and underground fliers; I could tell that Father didn't believe me, but I kept up the stories nevertheless, hoping that I could turn them into fact.

One evening my father bluntly started a conversation with my sister about the deportation night.

"Do you remember the SS man who took away Mother?" Father asked her abruptly.

"Of course," she answered. "I still remember his horrible, scarred face and the way he slapped me on the cheek. It was all red afterward.

"But Father," she continued, "how could you have seen him when you claim you didn't see us? If you saw the SS man who took away Mother, then you must have been with us. I was right next to Mother, pleading with him to let her go, which was when he slapped me."

Father became somewhat disoriented. "You see," he explained, "from where I was standing I could only see his profile. I never saw him head-on, nor was I able to distinguish the people he was selecting. They all looked alike. I may have seen Mother and not recognized her. But I was calling for both of you. Or maybe I imagine I was, maybe because of my fear I thought I was, but now I'm not sure any longer. One thing I'm sure of is that I wanted to shout, and that I meant to shout. But I don't even know if I made a sound. And this uncertainty is my constant nightmare.

"I saw multitudes of people, but I couldn't recognize any of them. My papers were never checked, and I wound up with the group to remain. I still don't know how it all happened. I think I was swept along with that mob that was already checked out, and nobody noticed. It was a miracle that I wasn't deported," he said. "Or maybe I shouldn't say that," he added.

My father sighed heavily and started wiping his eyes. My

sister took her coat and, without saying a word, went outside. It was past curfew. When I went after her she was standing in the dark hallway, crying.

"You are too hard on Father," I told her. "What are you trying to say with all this questioning?" I asked her.

"Don't you know? Do I have to spell it out for you? Unless you're too naïve to understand. I'm sure he abandoned us and saved himself," she answered through her tears as she walked to the other end of the hallway, sobbing.

I was dismayed. It felt as if someone had kicked me in the head; our father was not capable of such cowardice. I thought my sister was being dogmatic and unreasonable.

"Don't bother me anymore," she called over her shoulder.

"What's the point in torturing Father with all these questions?" I argued with her. "You know there wasn't a thing he could do to save Mother. Suppose he had gone, too. What good would that do us? Maybe I don't know what I'm talking about, but you ought to know, you were there. How could anybody save himself or anybody else? Wasn't it up to the Nazis whom to deport and whom to leave behind? You tried to intervene on Mother's behalf, and look what happened."

I could feel her tension and her pain. She stopped crying.

"Wasn't there something that kept telling you to save yourself?" I persisted. "Why did some people go into hiding and leave their families behind? Why the recriminations, why torture one another? What it comes down to is that we all want to stay alive. No one is guilty for it. Nor do we have the right to point fingers at anyone else."

"I just feel so sorry for Mother that she had to leave alone," my sister said, wiping her face. "If Father had gone with her, at least she wouldn't be alone, and that's what he should have done. She was his wife, and he owed it to her."

There was nothing else I could say. All I could do was to pity my father's predicament; it moved me to tears. I also realized how terribly we all missed Mother.

When I went back to the apartment Father was sitting on his iron cot reading a Nazi-controlled newspaper. "What is that you're reading?" I asked him. "Some more lies," he answered. "What's with your sister Hanka? Is she all right?"

"Yes," I said. "She needed some fresh air. It's so stuffy in here."

He gave me a funny look, the look he gave me when he didn't believe me, an expression I knew by heart.

The following day my father stayed home with a cold; normally he worked for the Nazis, moving and repairing furniture. That morning two armed Nazi gendarmes, assisted by several ghetto policemen, appeared in our yard escorting two young men. Father heard the commotion and looked out the window in time to witness some begging and pleading before the two men were placed against the brick wall of the adjoining building and shot point-blank from behind. When the shots rang out and the two men dropped to the ground Father nearly fainted, he told us that evening when we came home from work.

"This was the first time I ever witnessed an execution. It was a brutal, blood-chilling murder," Father said, shaking like a leaf. "I would never want to die in such a manner. God forbid," he said in an agitated voice.

"Do the Allies know what the Nazis are doing to us?" he asked me. In all my ignorance I assured him that they certainly knew and were only waiting for the right moment to strike back. Again he looked at me in disbelief, shaking his head. If he doubted my word, I wondered, why did he ask me such questions?

I remembered how two years earlier, when it was still possible, I had urged Father to leave Poland, but he had refused to listen. Instead he told me what World War I was like, and how much he had learned from it. "There is no sense running," he told me. "I have the experience. The best way is to stay put where your roots are." But two years later Father began to realize that this was a different war, a war against us, the Jews. By then it was too late; the borders were sealed.

When rumors started circulating about extermination

camps and gas chambers Father refused to believe them. He accused the doomsayers of spreading panic and demoralizing our poor, broken people.

"Not the Nazis, not even Genghis Khan himself would do such a thing," he would insist. "This is the twentieth century, and the civilized world would not allow it."

The Nazis kept up their brutal tactics; executions and roundups were a daily occurrence. People continued to disappear. To survive another day was a miracle.

On Sundays, when nobody went outside the ghetto to work, my father stood near the gate and watched the street outside. He stood there for hours at a time, sometimes past curfew, the cop on duty warned me. When I tried to tell Father how dangerous it was to stand near the gate he gave me a scornful look and said, "You told me that Mother would come back one day, so let me stand there and wait for her."

"Yes, I did say she would," I answered, "but nothing is certain, and no one knows for sure when or by what means people will return."

"Well, then," he said, "if you don't mind, I'll be standing right there by the gate whenever I can, and regardless of what people think."

Shortly after, Father was taken to the Szkolna labor camp next to the munitions plant at the other end of town. There was a shortage of labor, so the Nazis decided to replenish the Szkolna camp with people from the ghetto. Since I was still employed at the German-owned studio protected by the *Polizeiführer,* I remained in the apartment until the liquidation of the ghetto. During the winter of 1943, after an unsuccessful escape attempt, I was apprehended and shipped to the Maidanek extermination camp. I lost touch entirely with Father and my brother, who were together at the Szkolna camp. Only two years later, when the war was over, did I hear news of them.

On a hot August day in 1944, during the evacuation of the Szkolna camp to Germany, my father was ordered by the SS to get on a horse-drawn wagon marked with the Red Cross insignia, as were all other prisoners too weak to march any longer. Some minutes later the wagon turned off the road and drove into a clearing in the woods. Everyone on the wagon, including my father, was machine-gunned and buried in a mass grave nearby. My brother was a witness. My father was forty-eight years old.

THREE EGGS

Early in the fall of 1943, in the small ghetto of Radom, rumors circulated that the ghetto was about to be liquidated. No one knew when; even the police weren't sure, and they were nervous and agitated. I was waiting for my Polish underground contact to rescue me. They had told me how valuable I was to them and had promised to come. I had been involved with the underground for almost two years, passing to them important photographs I had been lifting from the studio where I worked.

One morning the Nazis rounded up four of us, put us on a truck, and drove off. They told us that we would be going to the Szkolna labor camp to pick up potatoes for the ghetto kitchen. Why did we have to get potatoes for the kitchen if the ghetto was about to be liquidated? This was a typical Nazi tactic: They tried to confuse us, and they always succeeded.

The Szkolna labor camp was located at the other end of the city, next to the munitions works. I knew my father was there—he had been transferred out of the ghetto some weeks before—so I was happy to be included in the mission. The driver took a shortcut through the back streets of the city, and

110

we soon arrived at the camp gate. The camp was guarded by heavily armed SS men who let us through. We were ordered to stay on the truck and not to talk to anyone.

It was a cold, rainy day; the area had turned to mud. There were several rows of wooden barracks with tiny windows. Small groups of prisoners carried cans of garbage; others rushed by without looking up. When the truck suddenly veered to the left most of us nearly fell off. The Nazi guards burst out laughing. I saw familiar faces, but nowhere did I see my father. The Nazis drove into an open area past the barracks, toward a warehouselike building. It stood all by itself in the middle of an empty field. Someone told me that inside this building the Nazis carried out executions.

The truck came to a stop, and we were ordered to enter the building at the lower level and carry bushels of potatoes out to the truck. As I was climbing back on the truck I noticed a group of men walking in our direction carrying shovels. Among them was my father. He saw me and signaled discreetly. I responded with a slight hand movement. As the truck started to roll into a U-turn we came a little closer to each other. Suddenly he reached into his pocket, quickly pulled out what looked like an egg, and threw it to me. At that moment the truck picked up speed; I leaned from the side but missed the catch. The egg fell to the ground. A guard ran over to my father and hit him on the head with a stick. There was nothing I could do. I saw his tears, but I was helpless. I wondered what he had had to sacrifice for that egg.

My father was in his late forties but now looked much older. He wore a dark gray three-quarter jacket with a gray scarf around his neck and an old battered hat. His stubbled face made him look old and sickly. His pants and shoes were covered with mud. On the way back to the ghetto I recalled the last Passover seder the family had spent together. One hard-boiled egg—the only egg we had—was cut into five portions and served with salt and water, a part of the traditional meal. There had been five of us, and my mother had divided the egg.

* * *

Bernard Gotfryd

Almost a year later I was myself a prisoner of the Nazis, working in Wieliczka, the oldest salt mine in Poland, not far from Krakow. The camp was located in an abandoned fruit orchard within walking distance of the mine. There were several hundred of us, including some women who were kept in separate barracks but worked with us in the mine. I worked the night shift 400 meters down, mixing and pouring cement floors. The mine was being converted into a Heinkel airplane-parts factory.

One evening, descending to the mine in a crowded elevator, a Polish miner in front of me gave me an egg. Polish miners were working on lower levels digging salt; sometimes we would ride the same elevators into the ground. I had never seen this man before; without saying a word he simply put the egg in the palm of my hand. As he got out of the elevator he turned around, winked at me, and walked away. I put the egg into my pocket, realizing I couldn't keep it there very long. The pockets of the camp uniforms were small; the egg would stand out, and eventually a guard would notice it. I decided to eat it that evening, right there in the mine during the break. In the meantime I had to hide it. This time, I told myself, I was not going to lose the egg.

Not far from the cement mixer where I worked was a pile of sand. I walked over, and when the guards looked away I stuck the egg into the very bottom of the pile. I noticed an indentation on the floor next to the spot that would serve as a marker. It was a good hiding place; I was sure no one had seen me, and that by the time the break was called the pile of sand would not yet have been used up.

For hours I stood at the mixer, feeding cement and pouring the ready mess into wheelbarrows. I realized that it had been more than a year since I had tasted a hard-boiled egg. I could picture peeling it and feeling the soft, smooth skin, the white, and finally the yolk. I had never liked egg yolk and wondered if I shouldn't trade it with someone for bread or half a bowl of soup. But how would I save the yolk and protect it from crumbling? I could save most of the shell in one piece and put

112

the yolk into it and carry it back to camp. How would I carry the egg without exposing it? I inquired around me, but in any event, no one had any extra bread to trade.

The break came, and I managed to retrieve the egg from the sandpile. I walked as far away from the mixer as was allowed and found a dimly lit corner. The moist air in the mine made me sleepy, and I felt weak in the knees. Leaning against a damp salt wall, I took out the egg. I still had a bit of bread left from my breakfast portion, and I decided to have it with the egg. The anticipation of such a feast was enough to give me gooseflesh. I was about to peel my egg when, out of nowhere, I heard a woman's voice; directly in front of me I saw an outstretched arm, long and thin. "Here is salt, but I have a sick sister. Wouldn't you share the egg with her?" I couldn't believe my eyes. I looked up and saw two big, shiny eyes staring at me. She stood there with her arm in the air, waiting. How was I going to share my egg? The idea was insane, I thought. Who was she, and how did she know I had an egg? In desperation I gave her the whole egg. "Give it to your sister. I hope she gets well." She took the egg and said, "God will repay you for such a noble deed, I'm sure." And as quietly as she had appeared, she walked away.

That was the second time I had lost an egg because I was clumsy and naïve. Soon the break was over, and I went back to mixing cement. I was hungry and frustrated, but I had managed to eat what was left of the bread. I felt some crumbs in my pocket and decided to leave them there. I would need them later.

The night shift was over; on my way to the elevator I noticed several dead bodies lying against the wall, waiting to be carried away. People were dying all the time from disease, starvation, or beatings. To my amazement, I noticed the woman to whom I had given the egg. She was lying on her back with her eyes wide open.

I wondered how she had died and what had happened to the egg. Had she given it to her sister? Someone told me that she was a former concert pianist, a survivor of the Warsaw ghetto uprising, and that her sister had been blown up inside a bunker defending the ghetto. I could hardly sleep. I envisioned the egg as the thing that had killed her. Maybe it was a bad egg, and she had eaten it. I felt a tremendous guilt; the scene with my father throwing the egg came back to haunt me.

Twenty years later I was married, I had two children, and I lived in an American suburb. My son belonged to the Cub Scouts. One summer, during a holiday weekend, parents were invited to participate in a scout picnic in one of the local parks. Fathers were asked to join their sons in different contests of skill. One contest consisted of two people throwing an egg back and forth, increasing the distance by a pace after each successful catch. It was a tricky game that required some dexterity, and I was happy to discover that my seven-year-old son was a talented catcher. For my part, I tried very hard. Everything went well for a while. Then I threw the egg, and it broke in my son's hand.

Some years later, when my son was in his teens, he recalled the episode, reminding me that it had been my fault. I accepted the blame easily, reassuring him that it had indeed been my clumsy handling of the egg that had caused it to break. I was in no mood to prolong any discussion of the scars ill-fated eggs had left on childhoods; I could see only my father tossing the egg, the dead woman lying on her back in the tunnel of the salt mine.

THE
EXECUTION

When the Szkolna camp was being evacuated in August 1944, before the onslaught of the Russian army, my father, who was one of the prisoners, was shot on the road not far from the city of Tomaszow. My brother, whom I did not see again until after the war, told me how it happened.

He had been with Father in the camp, and the two were together on the road. It was the height of summer, and the weather was warmer than usual at that time of year. There was no transportation, no water; marching in the heat was exhausting. Some people fainted and died. After several days of marching the SS men in command told them that if anyone felt tired, he should climb on the horse-drawn wagon marked with the Red Cross emblem that was following behind them.

Father, weak and exhausted from the long march, got on the wagon with some other people. Soon the Nazis drove the wagon off to a side road and into a clearing in the woods. My brother, sensing that something drastic was about to happen, ran after the wagon, begging the SS man in charge to release Father. The SS man pointed his rifle at my brother and threatened to shoot him unless he returned to the ranks. He knew the Nazi meant it; he did what he was told. Minutes later he heard terrible screams and a volley of rifle shots coming from the woods.

My brother told me he tried never to think about the incident; he felt very uneasy when he realized how helpless he had been. He asked me what I would have done in his place; I said I would most probably have taken a risk, though I wasn't really sure what exactly I would have done. Perhaps I could have saved Father. I was inclined to think that the Nazis, under very unusual circumstances, respected acts of courage. This is not to say that they didn't punish such acts with death, as happened in many cases of disobedience or open resistance. But they occasionally made exceptions.

Perhaps I was thinking of a particular morning during the winter of 1943–44 and a notorious death camp in eastern Poland, not far from Lublin. It was snowing lightly, and we were standing outside, several thousand of us, waiting to be counted, a daily routine. It was still dark; the reflectors surrounding the camp were on. Tiny snowflakes fell slowly, wetting my cheeks and settling on my eyelashes. That particular morning the count—or the *Appell,* as the Nazis called it—took longer than usual; the sick among us were beginning to faint and drop to the ground. We were not allowed to help them. They were to be left on the ground until after the *Appell,* when the death commandos would pick them up and cart them off to the crematorium.

Before long everything had turned white. The thousands of us that remained standing looked like puppets or rag dolls. It was an eerie picture: rows upon rows of silent, mismatched figures dressed comically in outdated military caps or tunics that were several sizes too small or too large.

Suddenly the SS guards brought in a gallows mounted on a flat truck and placed it in the center of the field. It was visible to everyone, lit by a huge reflector mounted on a utility pole. Four armed SS guards entered through the gate, escorting a man and a teenage boy dressed in striped prison uniforms with wooden clogs. The man was stooped and walked with a limp, supported by the teenager. They moved in the direction of the gallows. The camp commandant's voice came over the loudspeaker. He announced that an execution was about to take place, that the criminal about to be hanged had violated every camp rule, and that the teenager was his accomplice. The same treatment, he warned, awaited us as well if we didn't follow the camp rules.

I heard my own breathing and felt the stinging cold in my toes. I could clearly see the faces of the man and the teenager at the gallows. The man was middle-aged; he had heavy eyebrows, a strong face with high cheekbones. The teenager was thin, tall, handsome, probably only a little older than I. He stood at attention, looking straight ahead. As the two mounted the flat truck the man was pushed toward the gallows. He reached the assigned spot and bent over; abruptly two SS guards hoisted him on top of a stool. A third SS man fixed the noose around his neck. He wasn't blindfolded. When all was in place the SS guard in charge, a short, stocky man with a pockmarked face and an unusually dark complexion, mounted the truck and, with pistol in hand, ordered the teenager to kick the stool from under the man's feet. The teenager stared straight into the Nazi's eye but didn't move. I could see the Nazi's rage growing. He pulled the safety catch of his pistol and pointed it at the teenager's head. I was sure that a shot would follow and that that would be the end of the boy. The SS man was furious. He stamped his foot against the wooden platform, producing thudlike echoes. Foam formed on his mouth; like a wild animal he screamed at the teenager at the top of his lungs. It was impossible to understand a word of what he said. Then, unexpectedly, he put his pistol back in its holster and kicked the stool himself with his right foot; with a heavy blow to the teenager's body he pushed him to the ground.

The man dangled on the gallows, and suddenly the world around me was no longer the same. I felt a strange sensation in my throat as if I were choking. I could picture myself on the gallows, dangling in the air; I felt my spinal column getting

Bernard Gotfryd

longer and longer until it snapped in two. Once more the commandant's voice came over the loudspeaker; he assured us that the teenager would hang, too, but that first he would join a road-building gang, where they would teach him what hard work was all about.

By the time we walked back to the barracks it was daybreak, and the snow had stopped. High above me I could see the dissolving silver of the moon. As we entered the barracks I heard someone say, "Children, today is the first day of Chanukah, don't forget." I turned and saw a man, perhaps my father's age, his eyes still moist, his eyebrows white with frost, repeating over and over again, "Never forget this day, the twenty-seventh of Kislev, 5703. Never forget."

The following day my overseer, the German *kapo,* told me that the Nazi had spared the boy because he was impressed by his courage. Evidently it was something he felt only about this particular boy, for that same day the same Nazi had shot two prisoners for fighting over a cigarette butt he had thrown to the ground.

When the winter was over the Nazis evacuated the camp; some time later, after a short stay in the Wieliczka salt mines, I arrived in Mauthausen, Austria. While working in the stone quarry there I recognized the teenager from the other camp. He had survived the road gang and had also been shipped to Mauthausen. In the confusion of the evacuation they had forgotten about the promised hanging, he told me. I lost no time in letting him know how impressed I had been with his act of courage and how sorry I was about the hanging of his father.

This is what he said: "If I had kicked the stool out from under him, I would have been an accomplice to a murder. I couldn't do it; I believe in the Ten Commandments. The Commandment says, 'Thou shall not kill.' The man on the gallows was not my father, he was a stranger. We met in the camp; he treated me like a son, though, and wanted me to think of him as my father. My real father was killed by the Nazis two years before, trying to save my mother."

118

MY BROTHER'S
FRIEND

I remember Leon, my older brother's best friend, from my early childhood in Radom. When I walked by his father's monument shop on my way to school I would see him working with his father or stretched out on top of a tombstone reading a book.

Leon was short and muscular and had a pleasant disposition. I never saw him angry or upset; his eyes never failed to smile. At times he would allow me into his father's shop to watch him work, but as soon as his friends arrived he would ask me to clear out.

"You're too young to join us," he would say. "But you can come back after everyone goes." Sadly I would leave, waiting impatiently to grow older.

The monument shop was located on a narrow, hilly lot overgrown with tall grasses, weeds, and clusters of thorny purple thistle. At the far end a solitary willow tree cast a huge shadow across the grounds; tombstones of every imaginable size and shape stood everywhere. Large chunks of granite and marble chips were scattered about, giving the place the appearance of a vandalized cemetery.

To the right of the entrance stood a long wooden shed with faded red trim and two large, dusty windows; inside was a massive table loaded down with metal cans of paint and an array of paint-encrusted jars filled with worn-out brushes. Several old metal chairs leaned against the wall. Chisels and mallets and chains for hoisting and transporting tombstones hung from long, rusty hooks.

Sometimes I saw Leon's father moving slowly among the unfinished tombstones or checking inscriptions through a magnifying glass. In his left hand he held a thin brush; a metal tool protruded from the pocket of his blue apron, its sharp end reflecting in the sun. With the brush and the tool he would wipe dust off a stone or remove tiny specks of gold leaf from the narrow spaces between the lettering.

He was a soft-spoken man of medium height with a quizzical look on his face, as if he was trying always to suppress a smile. In my memory he wears a creased gray business suit, slightly frayed at the edges, a striped shirt with a loosely knotted polka-dot tie, and an old beige hat, its silk band stained with perspiration.

When Leon's friends weren't around I would watch him attentively as he chipped away at monuments. Tiny chunks of granite would scatter in all directions, covering a considerable distance. Leon wore a pair of goggles to protect his eyes from the dust and flying chips; I envied him the goggles and decided I would be either a monument-maker or a pilot when I grew up. I had seen pictures in movie magazines of actors portraying World War I pilots; how handsome and heroic they looked with their leather helmets and goggles and long white silk scarves flowing in the wind.

In the winter the monument lot was closed. Occasionally I would stop and peek through the cracks in the fence. Everything was covered with snow, and the bare willow looked as if it was curling up, shivering from the cold. Shaking in the wind, its ice-covered branches hung forlornly, as if begging to be brought back to life.

Half-buried in snow, the monuments with their carved

religious symbols looked like exotic birds suspended in space. One featured two human hands sculpted side by side, the fingers spread out in some odd symmetrical order. Another was carved in the shape of a tree cut in half. A black marble monument, slightly tilted, stood unsteadily in the middle of the lot. On its top two ornamental lions faced each other, their right paws slightly raised. Between them was a marble tablet with the Ten Commandments inscribed in gold.

The northern wind would blow in, shifting snowdrifts from one end of the lot to the other and whipping freshly fallen snow against the gravestones as if dressing them in white shrouds. As darkness fell and the silhouetted gravestones began to blend into the sky the lot would look ever more deserted and eerie.

Across the street from the monument lot an old man on crutches leaned against a whitewashed fence, trembling and shaking from the cold. Icicles grew off the ends of his white beard, and droplets of half-frozen tears stuck to his hairy cheeks. He wore an old, buttonless coat made up of tears and patches, and his legs were wrapped in layers of burlap tied together with bits of twine. Around his waist he had tied a heavy rope.

He was there every day throughout the year, and had been since I started going to school. Usually I would share my lunch with him, giving away one soft roll with jam. He couldn't eat crusty bread, he told me, for he had no teeth.

"Please help me pay for my gravestone," he begged year-round in a hoarse, breaking voice. "All I want is a stone with my name on it," he cried, blessing his givers—who were not legion—and promising them good health and long lives. Lowering his voice, he would berate the less generous, sending angry looks after them.

When things were slow at the monument lot Leon would sometimes pull over an old metal chair and start to chip away at a small headstone.

"Whose monument is that?" I asked one day, intrigued by its diminutive size.

"It belongs to Avrum the beggar, the one across the street. Some years ago he ordered his headstone, and he's been paying it off ever since. He told my father he knows that when he dies his only son, who is handicapped, won't be able to erect a tombstone for him, so he's decided to do it himself, while he's still alive. Given the circumstances, I can take my time and work on it at my leisure. It's a very inexpensive stone, but at the present rate it will still take him some years to pay it off."

Leon's eyes were focused on the stone he was carving. Soon his goggles were covered with a white layer of dust; large beads of perspiration began to appear on his forehead and cheeks, dripping ultimately to the ground. Leon turned around and, with an impatient gesture, whipped off his goggles and threw them to the ground.

"To hell with these goggles. Five minutes with them is all I can take. They fog up inside, they get dusty on the outside, and it's impossible to see with them."

He stood up, lit a cigarette, and blew a smoke ring. It floated upward, propelled by the slight breeze, vibrating and spreading out. I was in awe as I watched Leon blow one ring after another. I thought it was magic.

Some months later, during the summer of 1939, Avrum the beggar died, and Leon and his father erected the tombstone on his grave. Avrum was never able to complete his payments, I was told, but he got his tombstone nevertheless.

September came, and World War II broke out. When the Nazis occupied our city they confiscated all Jewish-owned properties, including the monument shop. Most of Leon's father's stones were carted away to be used as steps for an office building the Nazis were erecting in our city.

For many reasons I lost track of Leon and didn't see him until late in 1943, when we met in a cattle car on the way to the Maidanek concentration camp. The car was packed, stuffy, and hot. What normally would be a three-hour trip took us two days and two nights. Only the sick and the elderly were allowed to sit on the floor of the car; Leon and I stood up for most of the trip, talking. I felt safe next to him. He was protective of me and treated me like his younger brother. I was eighteen, and Leon was in his twenties, my older brother's age.

"We are trapped with no chance to escape," Leon told me, "and even if we succeed in escaping there is nowhere to go. We're surrounded by the enemy. They are everywhere."

In Maidanek Leon and I wound up working in the same commando, taking apart old machinery parts for scrap. Shortly before Easter of 1944 *kapo* Fritz asked me if I knew how to paint Easter cards. "The SS camp commandant," he said, "is looking for an artist who knows how to paint Easter cards."

"I don't know how to paint," I told him, "but I have a friend who does." The following day Leon and I set up shop. We got paints, brushes, and lots of white paper for making envelopes; we were given a small cubicle with a rickety crate for a table in a barrack next to the *kapo's* quarters. Two smaller crates served as chairs; we also had a bunk bed. We were excused from our everyday duties and were confined to the cubicle for as long as it might take to produce several hundred Easter cards.

Leon set out to paint tiny yellow chicks peeking out of cracked eggshells; I was to cut the cards to size and produce envelopes. The room was very small, and in no time at all our double bunk and the floor were covered with freshly painted cards.

Kapo Fritz became our official overseer. He was tall, fat, and very blond. His eyes were a watery blue; everything else about him seemed colorless. He came from Berlin, he told us, where the most decent Germans come from. *Kapo* Fritz became a constant visitor, appearing when least expected, but never forgetting to bring hot soup or coffee and new card orders with him.

Leon was original and creative. He combined chicks with

ducklings; he decorated the cracked eggshells with faces of smiling children. I pointed out to him that chicks and ducklings didn't mix, but he just laughed off the comment. At the back of my mind I had a recurrent vision of myself dangling from the gallows next to Leon.

One morning we heard a commotion outside our door. Suddenly a tall, fat man in an SS uniform with lots of silver trim appeared inside our room. We jumped to attention and froze. It was the commandant of the camp about whom we had heard so many dreadful stories. With him was the "gypsy," his assistant, who purportedly used prisoners for target practice.

The camp commandant spoke to Leon, addressing him as *Herr,* and ordered him to paint fifty additional cards that would be signed with the commandant's initials, as if he himself had painted them. He ordered the "gypsy" to see that Leon and I got better clothing and leather shoes and asked *kapo* Fritz to get rid of our wooden clogs. Leon was still thanking him when the "gypsy" turned and hit Leon in the face with his fist.

As soon as they left I went to the sink to wet a clean rag for Leon, whose nose was bleeding profusely. When I returned Leon was laughing hysterically; tears were rolling down his cheeks. "It could have been worse," he gasped through tears. "He could have killed us. Look, we are still alive! Let's get back to work. We've just won the lottery," he said.

After midnight that same evening, on my way down the long corridor that led to our toilet, I made a mistake and opened the wrong door. I found myself inside a nearly dark room. A ray from the moving searchlights came through the window, shedding enough light for me to make out the contents of the room. Cartons with Red Cross labels were stacked neatly against the walls. In one corner of the room stood several open cartons. I put my hand inside one and found a can of sardines, bread, apples, and cookies. Silently I filled my pockets, and I left the room as quickly as I could. When I returned to our cubicle Leon was still hard at work.

"We have deadlines," he announced jokingly, "and they must be met, or else. You'd better make some more envelopes if you want to live another day."

I silenced him with a cookie; he couldn't believe our good fortune. We stayed up late, and in the dark we ate up my find.

"To die from hunger is very undignified," Leon asserted. An apple pip dropped to the floor and rolled under the bunk. Leon went after it, stuck it in his mouth, and chewed it to a paste.

"We can't afford to leave the slightest trace, not even an apple pip. If they knew that we helped ourselves to that food, that would be our end," Leon said. The sugar-covered cookies were especially delicious; we checked everywhere for crumbs.

The following night I ventured back for more food. In my stocking feet, so as not to make any noise, I tiptoed into the miracle room, as it seemed at the time. We still had several days of work left, Leon had figured; every night I went back down the hall for more provisions, disregarding the risks involved.

The food parcels, we found out later, were sent to some Polish prisoners through the International Red Cross, but none of the prisoners for whom they were intended was alive any longer. Since the *kapos* helped themselves to the food, we hardly felt bad about sharing it with them.

One morning Leon noticed a small group of women prisoners walking along a path not far from our little window. They were better dressed than the rest of the inmates; some even wore winter coats, a rarity among prisoners. Before they disappeared behind the barracks Leon said, "No, this is impossible, that couldn't be my cousin Ilka."

He then told me about a favorite female cousin of his who had disappeared during the deportations two years earlier. No one had heard news of her since.

Kapo Fritz came in with a pot of hot coffee. "Just a few minutes ago," Leon told him, "I saw a group of nicely dressed women outside the window. Who are they?"

Fritz started laughing. "They are the ladies from the Puffhouse," he answered. "Just down the road is a little Puffhouse, and every morning our ladies go to the showers. They must keep clean for the SS guards and some privileged *kapos* like myself," he boasted, still laughing.

With Fritz's help Leon ascertained that the young woman was indeed his lost cousin. One morning Fritz even arranged for Leon to speak to her on her way to the showers. He escorted her to the window of our room, where Leon was able to talk to her while Fritz stood behind her, shielding her from view.

Ilka was a pretty blond girl who had a small, sweet face with full red lips, blue eyes, and a pale complexion. She couldn't have been more than eighteen. She wore a black beret, a short black winter coat, and a white woolen scarf.

She recognized Leon immediately. He stood staring at her, bewildered and embarrassed. He looked at her as if he had never seen her before; every time he tried to say something, strange sounds came out of him. Finally he managed a start.

"I was really worried about you, Ilka. How are you?" he asked. "Just fine," she answered, smiling sadly at him and showing a full mouth of beautiful teeth. One wondered how it was possible to look so healthy in such a dreadful, wretched place.

I heard her ask him, "Do you need anything, Leon? Can I get you some food or a shirt, shoes perhaps. . . . Look, don't be bashful. . . . I can help you. I have friends." And she told him how well off she was and said he shouldn't worry about her.

"Don't worry about me," she kept assuring him, smiling.

"What made you do this? Why?" he asked her, and his face turned white. He was trembling as if he had a fever.

"I had no choice," she said. "I didn't want to starve to death. I'd rather be humiliated than go hungry. I couldn't stand being hungry any longer. Please don't talk about me. Try to understand me. I'm fine."

Kapo Fritz became nervous when he noticed an SS man walking toward us. He motioned to Ilka to finish the conversation, took her by the arm, and escorted her across the frozen ground to the group of women. Quickly they marched off to the showers. The SS man paid no attention and disappeared behind the row of barracks.

This was the last time Leon saw his cousin Ilka. Some days later *kapo* Fritz brought him a can of sardines from her and told him that she had been shipped out to a different camp. Soon afterward we heard rumors that all the Puffhouse women had been exterminated. This was how the Nazis took care of their Puffhouse ladies when they became sick or got pregnant.

Some weeks later, in the spring of 1944, when the Nazis evacuated Maidanek, Leon and I were shipped out in two separate transports. In the late summer of 1944 we met again in a camp called Gusen, in Austria.

Leon wasn't the man I had known. I hardly recognized him; he was sickly-looking, and his spark was gone. He kept staring at me with expressionless eyes, as if he didn't know who I was. He couldn't get over Ilka's fate and kept asking me, "Why did they have to kill her? Why?"

I kept assuring him that he must be mistaken, that Ilka had to be alive, that the Nazis wouldn't kill such a beautiful girl. But I knew better.

The winter of 1944–45 was very cold. It snowed constantly, and everything turned into one thick sheet of ice. The conditions in Gusen were abominable, and there was an acute food shortage. We worked long shifts at the underground Messerschmitt plant. Typhoid and dysentery epidemics raged out of control, and the Nazis did nothing about them. They just let us die.

There wasn't much I could do for Leon but feed him lies and encouragement and try to make him eat his soup. He wasn't hungry anymore, he told me; he was only cold. His eyes were getting larger, and his bony blue face was getting thinner. Finally he refused to eat, and it became difficult to communicate with him. He was shrinking by the minute.

"Do you remember Avrum the beggar?" Leon asked me one morning on the way to the plant. "He is a lucky man," he said. "He has his tombstone on his grave."

Leon and I had survived several camps together, but Gusen was the last. At Gusen he was beaten to death by a *kapo* who accused him of stealing another inmate's jacket. It was established later that Leon had stolen nothing. The inmate had traded his jacket to Leon for a bowl of soup, but, afraid of being punished for losing the jacket, he had blamed Leon for stealing it.

More than two decades later I went to California to visit a friend who convinced me to join him at a gathering of Holocaust survivors.

At the gathering I immediately noticed a very beautiful woman. I knew that I had seen her before but could not remember where. I kept following her with my eyes; when she stopped to talk to another woman not far from where I was standing I recognized her voice. It was Ilka's voice, resonant and high-pitched; I remembered it distinctly.

She had put on weight, her blond hair had turned darker, and her sad eyes were not the blue I had glimpsed through the window in Maidanek. I could hear her conversation: She was telling her friend about a camp she was sent to where the Nazis used her for medical experiments, and how as a result of it she still suffered from excruciating migraine headaches. I heard the other woman call her Ilka; I waited patiently, hoping to hear more, but Ilka talked only about the experiments and not about Maidanek.

As soon as her companion walked away I went over to her and introduced myself.

"Excuse me," I said, "but I wonder if you are by any chance related to Leon G." Upon hearing her cousin's name she turned pale. For a few seconds she just looked at me, and then, carefully enunciating every word, she began to talk.

"Yes, as a matter of fact I am related to Leon G., and I am still trying to find out what happened to him. In all these years I have never met anybody who knew him or was with Leon in the camps. But who are you? Were you with him?"

"Leon was my brother's friend in Radom," I told her. "I knew him most of my life. I was with him in Gusen."

I really wasn't sure what I was doing or whether I was saying the right thing. I decided not to mention Maidanek; I had a feeling that she didn't want anybody to know about her time there. I only hoped that she wouldn't remember me. Possibly she had never noticed me standing next to Leon when he talked to her through the window in Maidanek. Or was she playing my game, pretending that there was no Maidanek?

My awkwardness grew. I told Ilka briefly what had happened to Leon in Gusen, and her eyes filled with tears. She reached inside her bag and pulled out a pack of tissues. Slowly she wiped her tears, excusing herself for acting like a child.

"I am sorry," she said quietly, "but I liked Leon a lot."

"I did, too," I answered honestly.

As she was about to leave me she turned quickly and asked point-blank: "How did you know I was related to Leon?"

"Somebody in New York—I forget who—described you to me and told me you were Leon's relative," I lied again.

"You have a very good eye. Yes, it's true. I am his only living relative," she answered, almost proudly. Smiling sadly, she shook my hand before walking away to join her woman friend.

HANS BÜRGER
#15252

I first saw Hans Bürger in Maidanek, a notorious concentration camp near the city of Lublin in eastern Poland. He was a robust man, perhaps in his forties or older, with a neck and cheeks as red as those of a Prussian officer, which he claimed he had been during World War I. He was partially bald and had a perfectly round, meaty face with blue eyes and bushy, graying eyebrows. It was unusual for a prisoner to look so well after so many years in the camps—this was Bürger's sixth year of incarceration, my friend Eddie told me. When Hans Bürger walked he nearly marched, torso aligned, his arms swinging. It was difficult to understand why a man like him was rotting away in the camps, though we assumed he was there for the same reason the rest of us were.

Hans worked as a clerk at the camp's main office and shared a small cubicle with another German prisoner. He even wore a wristwatch—an unheard-of privilege inside a camp. His striped uniform was made of better-quality fabric, and his leather shoes were always immaculate. Even his prisoner number had been embroidered on his tag. Hans Bürger was the envy of every prisoner and *kapo* in Maidanek.

HANS BÜRGER

In the spring of 1944, during the evacuation of Maidanek, I came in direct contact with Hans; we shared the same cattle car. He sat on the floor a few feet from me, surrounded by a group of prisoners. His canvas sack stood on the floor next to him. It was hard to imagine what could be in it. He was probably the only prisoner to carry a bag. None of the rest of us had anything to carry outside of a tin bowl and a spoon, if that much.

Early on in the trip Hans took off his jacket, neatly folded it inside his sack, rolled up his shirtsleeves, and, unexpectedly, started lecturing us about hygiene, germs, and diseases. He seemed uncomfortable to be closed in tightly with so many people who spoke Polish or Yiddish, languages he didn't understand. Before the train started moving the only slop pail for the entire car began to overflow, which annoyed Hans no end. Pointing to the pail, he tried to impress upon us how dangerous it could be to ignore sanitary rules, but few listened.

It was hot and stuffy in the car, but Hans kept busy stopping fistfights, which were breaking out at a faster rate than he was able to handle. People were commenting to one another about Hans's nerve, trying to preach to us about things like hygiene when we were hungry and didn't know where the Nazis were taking us. Most of us seemed to be intimidated by his interference, but only one man dared to tell him as much: Shlomo the baker. Shlomo was a husky man in his late thirties, tall, wiry, and impulsive. He had fought in the Warsaw ghetto uprising, he told us; he was only sorry that the uprising hadn't lasted longer. "If we had only had more weapons," Shlomo would reminisce, "we could have given the Nazis real hell."

Suddenly Shlomo, who was standing near the window, started pushing his way through the crowd toward Hans. He stopped in front of Hans and asked him, in very good German, "Sir, who authorized you to be our leader and arbitrator? Don't you think we should first take a vote, or at least put up another candidate? We're a majority here, and most of us don't even speak your language."

"Why, you idiot!" Hans shouted back. "If you have any objections, then you take over. Show us what you can do, if you're so smart. Do you really think I like to do this? It's all yours. Take it, be the leader, and stop intimidating me."

Shlomo, visibly annoyed at Hans's diatribe, shouted back at him, "As soon as you open your mouth you insult me, and then you have the nerve to accuse me of intimidating you. How typical. Just because you're a German Jew, you think you're smarter and more cultured than the baker from Poland. If you're so smart, then why are you here with us? Tell me, please." Hans scratched the back of his head impatiently, waiting for Shlomo to finish.

"If you insist, I'll tell you," Hans shouted back at Shlomo, his face beet-red. "First of all, I'm older than most of you here, and I would like to ask you for some respect. Nobody will talk down to me. I happen to have been a lieutenant in the German army during World War I. I am also a recipient of the Iron Cross, first class, for bravery." Hans stopped talking. "Just a moment," he said, reaching into his shirt pocket. He pulled out a tiny bundle wrapped in gray tissue paper; from it he produced a miniature black cross with shiny edges.

"You thought I was telling you a fairy tale," he continued. "Here it is, look. I earned it by putting my life on the line. I was even wounded, and I've suffered, but this is what one must do for one's country." He showed the Iron Cross to a few curious ones. Seemingly satisfied with the silence, he proceeded to rewrap the tiny cross.

"So this, I hope, should give you an idea that I have some experience, and I know what war is. And now let me tell you why I'm here. I'm here because of a clerical mistake made in Berlin some years ago by some dumb bureaucrat. Let me assure you that as soon as we arrive at our destination that mistake will be rectified, and I'll be out of here. The camp commandant in Maidanek personally assured me that he has taken actions on my behalf. Germany won't let me down, and

132

this I'm sure of. I fought for Germany; now Germany will fight for me."

With trembling hands Hans replaced the tiny package in his shirt pocket; he then secured the pocket with a safety pin. "Herr Lieutenant," Shlomo asked quietly, "would you care to tell us how you were able to smuggle that Iron Cross into camp? Did you have to hide it in your rectum, by any chance?"

Hans, obviously insulted, shouted back, "No, you cretin, I wore it proudly in my lapel when I was first brought to camp but was advised to hide it so that people like you couldn't steal it from me. I hope you're satisfied."

"No wonder you're so sure of yourself," Shlomo answered, smiling. "You shit Iron Crosses. That's why. You'll see how Germany will fight for you, just give them enough time. I don't understand how a man with your intelligence can go on believing such dreck. You seem to forget that according to the Nuremberg law you're a Jew, and as such you're doomed like the rest of us. Believe me, I'm not trying to spoil it for you, but do me a favor, don't show off your moldy Iron Cross to me; I'm not impressed."

Hans was exasperated. Large beads of perspiration were running off his face. He didn't answer Shlomo but glared at him with disdain, then turned his back. There was perfect silence in the car; you could hear only the monotonous sound of the wheels knocking against the seams of the tracks, a perfect reminder of the uneasy peace inside the cattle car. Shlomo pushed his way to the barred window at the back of the car and stretched out on the floor underneath it.

Soon night fell. Hans was curled up in a sitting position, his head resting on his knees. Others stood or sat on the floor, supporting each other back to back. Before long the car was filled with sounds of snoring and moaning. I sat next to the door, not far from Hans, leaning with my face against the crack and gasping for fresh air. I still had a little bread left, as well as some water Anton had given me before I left

Maidanek. I wet my parched lips with a few drops of the lukewarm water left in the canteen and took a small bite of bread. I couldn't sleep. I peeked out through the crack in the door and tried to locate the Big Dipper, but I wasn't successful; we were going south, and I was facing west. The sky seemed to be filled with billions of stars. I hoped one would fall so I could make a wish. From time to time, in the darkness of the night, I would see a blinking light. The train would slow down to switch tracks or to let another train go by. Now and then the locomotive would let out an ear-piercing whistle, waking up everybody in the car. "Did we arrive yet?" people would ask, half asleep.

With the first rays of dawn Hans started moving. He opened his eyes, rubbed his cheeks, and got to his feet. He started stretching his arms and twisting his body sideways, his hands on his hips. When I turned to watch he spoke to me: "It's good for you to do some calisthenics, my friend, especially in the morning when you get up from sleep. It's very healthy for you, you know?" I started moving my arms alongside him until I had worked up a sweat. Hans looked at me approvingly and asked me if it felt any better. "Yes," I said, "much better." "You must exercise a little," Hans repeated, moving closer to the door where I was standing.

"It's so much nicer here with this wide crack in the door and all the fresh air you get. You have the best spot in the whole car, away from the troublemakers, like the one over there," he said, pointing in the direction of the window, where Shlomo was still stretched out on the floor. Hans noticed my water canteen. "You must not waste a single drop of water," he said, looking straight at me. "You must always remember that a transport may take three to five days, and so you must make the water last all that time. It takes discipline and willpower. But above all, you must be selfish if you want to survive." I thanked him for his advice, and he moved back to his spot. He took a neatly wrapped slice of bread out of his sack and ceremoniously began to break off small pieces. He offered me a piece of bread, but I declined. "I still have some of my own,"

I told him. He chewed the bread slowly, as if trying to make it last forever.

Not long into the morning a fight broke out near where Hans sat. "Look, you fools," Hans started lecturing, "this is really what the Nazis want you to do. They dehumanize you so you can kill each other, and you probably will. Why don't you use your heads?" Sheepishly the two men stopped fighting. Shlomo stood at the window, deep in thought, looking at nothing in particular; a sadness emanated from him.

Rifle shots rang out, and the train started slowing down. We dropped to the floor, almost on top of one another. The train came to a full stop; there was lots of shouting and more rifle fire. I heard doors slide in other cars and a good deal of commotion.

After a few minutes our doors were unlocked; one by one we were ordered outside to be counted. Two SS men entered our car and started checking the floorboards, which were all in place. Then it was back into the car on the double. We started climbing over one another desperately, only to be pulled back from behind by others. The two SS men stood on each side of the door, amusing themselves by hitting us with heavy sticks. The screams of pain were horrifying; so were the sounds of cracking bones. Exhausted and bleeding, we all managed to get back into the car.

As we were getting resettled the SS officer in charge of the transport appeared in front of our open door and called out for Hans Bürger. Eagerly Hans, a smile on his face, came forward and jumped off the car. Straight as a nail he stopped in front of the officer. *Wer bist du?*—Who are you?—the SS officer asked him. "Lieutenant Hans Bürger, a recipient of the Iron Cross, first—" Hans began, but he wasn't given a chance to finish the sentence. Like a thunder the SS officer's gloved fist came down on Hans's face; Hans crumpled to the ground. *"Aufstehen, aufstehen, schnell"*—Get up, get up, fast—the SS officer shouted, kicking him, as Hans struggled to his feet. His face was a bloody mess.

"And now do you know who you are? You swine," the

officer shouted at Hans, only inches from his face. "I'm prisoner swine #15252, Herr Sturmführer," Hans answered, his voice breaking. The SS officer pulled out a pistol and put it to Hans's temple, shouting, "Next time I won't ask any questions." He kicked him hard and walked off to the front of the train. We all stood watching this humiliating scene. As soon as Hans was helped back into the car the sliding door was shut and bolted with a screeching noise; the train continued on its way.

Hans stretched out on the floor, a defeated man. He covered his swollen face with both hands and, turning to face the door, started sobbing. Several of us looked at one another in sympathy. This must have been the worst humiliation any man could endure, especially one who had thought himself special so recently.

Shlomo reappeared from the other end of the car, limping, with a towel around his neck. On his knees he began wiping Hans's face. "Let me help you, my friend, if you don't mind me calling you that. I'm all right," Shlomo said. "The SS bastards didn't get me; I just hurt my leg getting back in the car, but look what they did to you. They'll be punished for it, don't worry, my friend." Hans didn't resist or make a sound. Shlomo's kindness caught us all by surprise. It was a strange sight, the former enemies in so intimate a pose. Some people offered Hans bread and water, but he refused to accept it. He had enough of his own, he indicated.

The train was stopping and slowing down as if it wasn't sure which way to go. Someone at the far end of the car found out why we had stopped and been counted, and why the SS guards had tested the floorboards in every car. He had overheard a conversation between two SS guards when we were outside.

"In one of the cars ahead of ours," he told us, "some people managed to lift two loose floorboards. When the train slowed down at a curve they lowered themselves down and dropped to the ground between the tracks. Ten people got out, but only one managed to escape. When the train picked up speed the SS guards on the roof of the last car noticed them and started shooting. Those were the rifle shots we heard before. Nine dead bodies were carried back to the same car from which they escaped."

"To think that a German could brutalize one of their own in front of so many people," somebody in the car commented, obviously more taken aback by the indignities Hans had suffered than by this news.

"Are you surprised?" a voice in the back answered. "How long have you been in the camps, my friend? They specialize in dehumanizing and degrading people, regardless of nationality. You talk about brutality. . . . Did you ever witness a hanging?"

There was silence; no one dared say anything more. The *ta-ta-tam, ta-ta-tam* of the wheels against the tracks again echoed loudly.

Shlomo and Hans now stood near me, next to the door. "Don't worry, Lieutenant," Shlomo was saying, a hand on Hans's shoulder. "To me and the rest of us here you're Lieutenant Hans Bürger, who won the Iron Cross for bravery. I think you're a brave gentleman, and I'm sorry for having insulted you, Herr Lieutenant." Hans lifted his head, attempting a smile; his swollen face managed only a contorted expression of grief.

Someone at the back of the car announced that we were nearing Krakow. It didn't matter to any of us anymore where we were going, as long as Hans stopped sobbing. Covering his swollen face with one hand, he turned around to face the silent crowd behind him. "I just want to tell you what decent fellows you are," he said. "I'll never forget you." He shook Shlomo's hand.

Shlomo slapped him lightly on the shoulder before making his way to the barred window to see if we were really nearing the city. A few hours later we indeed arrived at Plaszow, not far from Krakow. In Plaszow our transport was separated; some of us stayed, others were shipped elsewhere. Here I lost track of both Hans and Shlomo.

* * *

Several months later, in Mauthausen, a man I carried rocks with told me he had known Hans Bürger in a camp before Hans arrived at Maidanek. Hans was not a Jew, he said, but was married to a Jewish woman with whom he had two children. Shortly before the war Hans was able to get his family out of Germany to Switzerland, but when he returned to Germany to see his sick mother he was arrested by the Gestapo. He subsequently wound up in Maidanek.

Out of empathy, the man said, Hans masqueraded as a Jew; he helped Jews whenever he could, never made an issue of it, and made a point of not talking to anyone about his private life.

THE LAST
CAMP

In August of 1944, after three weeks of hard labor at the Mauthausen stone quarry—three weeks of climbing one hundred and twelve steps six times daily with a heavy rock on my bare shoulders—I was shipped to the Messerschmitt plant at Gusen II, in Austria.

Gusen II was a fairly small camp set in a valley, surrounded by farmland. Outside the electric wire fence was a desolate perimeter bordered by another double wire fence; the concentric ring formed a corridor wide enough for the guards to patrol. The camp had eight watchtowers manned by SS guards with mounted machine guns. Far away, beyond the emptiness, one could see green fields with small clusters of trees silhouetted against the horizon.

Upon my arrival at the plant I became a planer operator. I'll never know what made the Nazis think I could do the job. In three months of trying to grasp the intricacies of the machine, as well as learning how to deal with the idiosyncrasies of my Nazi supervisors, I caused incalculable damage to the Third Reich by breaking a great many vanadium-steel-tipped knives.

Vanadium, I was told, was the hardest steel in existence, and it was very expensive to manufacture.

The screeching of the planers, plus the adjacent lathe and drilling machines and several rows of sheet-metal workers who kept dropping aluminum and steel plates on top of a pile, created such a high-decibel noise that it was impossible to bear. I remember stuffing my ears with little balls of soft bread. The Nazis and the technical personnel plugged their ears with cotton or avoided the area whenever possible.

By autumn the Messerschmitt management had reason to be concerned about the diminishing labor force at the plant. Between recurrent epidemics of typhoid and dysentery and a chronic lack of nourishment, workers were disappearing faster than they could be replaced. Productivity was lagging far behind quota.

One day my supervisor, Herr Gruber, sorely tried by my performance with the planer but impressed by my proficiency in the German language, recommended me to head a food commando that the Messerschmitt management was about to set up. I suspected that this was his revenge for all the vanadium knives I'd managed to break.

In order to reverse the downward trend the Messerschmitt management offered food supplements to the most productive workers at the plant, or about ten percent of the work force. The food had to be brought in from the nearby Messerschmitt warehouse in St. Georgen. With the help of four Russian prisoners, a wagon with crates for the bread, two thermal tanks for the soup, and two SS guards to watch over it all, I was to do the job. Twice weekly we set off for the warehouse, brought back food to the plant, cut the bread, and distributed it according to lists drawn up by the plant supervisors. The final distribution of the food to the prisoners was done by a Russian POW, Andrei, and his assistants.

On my second trip to the warehouse I realized how easy it was to add more soup and loaves of bread to our wagon without incurring any great risks. So I added quantities of food and began passing on the extra portions to each listed

department. In such a manner some prisoners who were not
on the list were getting extra food. They wondered why, but
they weren't complaining.

Early one morning, as we were walking over a frozen field of
ice-covered furrows to the train that would take us to work,
my foot caught inside a rut, and I twisted my ankle. Almost
immediately I started limping; I feared the injury would put
me in sick bay, which could be the end of me.

In the pre-dawn darkness I heard someone ask in Russian,
"What happened to your foot?" When I looked behind me I
saw a broad-shouldered man of medium height dressed in a
striped prisoner's uniform. In Gusen everybody wore the
same uniforms. He moved closer as I tried to tell him in the
little Russian I had picked up in Maidanek that my foot was
hurting. It was still too dark for me to be able to distinguish
his features, but I could tell he was older than I. He asked the
man next to him to help him lift me by my elbows; he asked
me to fold and stiffen my arms and make myself as light as
possible. In this way I was carried into the train and from the
train to the plant.

I had no idea what made the Russian help me. Normally
very few people went out of their way to help others unless
they were of the same nationality. He and the other man
carried me inside the plant through the long underground
tunnel and deposited me at my station in front of the planer.
As I was adjusting my machine another Russian prisoner
whom I had never seen before came by and quickly handed
me some chunks of ice wrapped inside a wet, torn sock. He
told me to apply it to my ankle right away.

"Andrei said you must," he whispered in Russian, and he
walked to his station.

My ankle was badly swollen, and I was in a good deal of
pain; still I was intent on hiding my injury from the Nazis.
The dour Herr Gruber kept casting glances at me as if he
suspected something. I kept busy, pretending to focus my eyes
on the moving knife and watching him at the same time. I

didn't think Herr Gruber was a bad man, after all. Some weeks earlier I had found half a sausage and a slice of white bread inside a pocket of my French military tunic, which hung on the wall not far from his desk at the plant. Best of all, the sausage was wrapped in an undated German newspaper clipping announcing the Allied invasion of Normandy. I spent a long time trying to figure out how far it was from Normandy to Gusen; I hated to think how long it would take the Allies to travel more than a thousand kilometers. After secretly reading the newspaper clipping I hid it inside my shoe. Soon it disintegrated to a pulp, but I left it there, hoping the news would keep my foot warm.

Only Herr Gruber could have put the newspaper-wrapped sausage in my pocket. Herr Gruber rarely talked; he did so, in fact, only when he screamed at me for breaking a knife. I had trouble figuring him out. In particular I wondered if he had paid attention to his wrapping materials; did he want me to know about the Allied invasion?

Who was Andrei, and why did he care to help me? I wondered about that most of the day as I watched the tip of the knife whittling away at a row of steel brackets and tried to forget my ankle. In the afternoon, after the soup break, the Russian who had brought me the chunks of ice stuffed inside a sock returned with more. He left the sock on the floor beside me and, without saying a word, walked away. Luckily, Herr Gruber was not at his desk.

Then came the shrill whistle, and it was time to go back to camp. I wondered how I would manage, but as soon as I stopped the machine I felt myself lifted off the floor by two Russians who appeared from nowhere. In the same manner as before they carried me outside, discreetly holding me under my elbows. Surrounded by hundreds of prisoners marching in ranks of five, we made it through the gate and into the train. It was a short ride back to camp, only fifteen to twenty minutes.

On the train I found myself standing between Andrei and his friend Dimitri and was at last able to get a good look at them. Andrei had a strong face with high cheekbones, a broad chin, and quiet gray eyes, unless the dim light inside the train was altering their color. There was something good and reassuring about him. It was difficult to determine his age, but he seemed to be in his mid-thirties. In camps people were aging fast and looked much older than they were in reality. Dimitri, his friend, was taller, thinner, very blond, and very shy. I didn't know what to say to them and very apologetically, in the best Russian I could muster, thanked them for being so kind to me. Turning my head from one to the other, I blurted out: "Thank you very much. It's very unusual what you are doing for me. I'm very grateful." Andrei looked at me, and his face lit up: "When the time comes we want you to be able to go home without a limp, because somebody will be there waiting for you. Don't worry about the ankle. All you have to do is keep applying the ice, and soon you'll be well again."

Dimitri was quiet. He offered me a drag of a thumbnail-sized cigarette butt he had pulled out of his pocket and lit; immediately my head began to spin. It must have been a camp cigarette made from some strange mixture of herbs. Andrei didn't smoke.

When we arrived in camp it was nearly dark. People were rushing in and out of the barracks, trading their bread rations for cigarettes or their clothing for bread or soup. Loud bargaining could be heard over some more complex transactions. Almost everybody had something to trade; of the babble of languages Russian could be heard most of all.

One Sunday, my day off, I was walking behind the barracks looking for a sunny spot to rest when I saw Andrei approaching me. "I would like to see you for a moment. It's such a beautiful day. Let's sit down in the sun and talk," he said in his clear, accentuated Russian. Some months had gone by, and I now had a better command of Russian.

"Young man," Andrei addressed me, "I'll get to the point. There isn't much time to talk. We like people like you who don't mind taking risks. And so I must tell you that we've watched you for a long time with your bread scheme, and we've come to the conclusion that you are one of us. That means that we trust you and would like you to join us. Many months ago, long before you arrived, we started organizing. You may call it a conspiracy, if you like. When the right time comes we must be ready to take over the camp in order to prevent a slaughter. You must understand that when we become useless the Nazis will destroy us. Did you know that more than thirty thousand Russian prisoners of war and many thousands of others died here building the Messerschmitt plant? We aren't willing to share their fate, not if we can help it, and we think we can help it. When we have rifles we will win. You see, we all have somebody back home. I have a wife and two little boys, parents and brothers and sisters—a big family, and I'm sure they're waiting for me. So I plan on going back. Did you understand everything I'm saying? If not, you can ask me questions."

I was flabbergasted. "Frankly," I answered, "I don't know what to say. I'm honored that you trust me. I really don't know what I can do for you—even if you want me to do anything at all—but I'll do whatever you ask. I also have a family that I would like to see again, but above all I would like to see the end of that monster. You know who I mean, don't you?"

Andrei nodded. "Yes, yes, I know. But I must go now," he said, and, lowering his voice, he continued: "Just keep supplying the bread so our people can stay alive. We have over two hundred people to worry about, and some aren't so healthy anymore. Every extra drop of soup or slice of bread is a big help. So far as I can tell, the Nazis don't know a thing about the bread scheme, and my people certainly won't tell, even if they're strung up. The only person that worries me is that new arrival who speaks Russian with a German accent. He claims to be a Czech. He just walks around and snoops. I never see him do any work. Very suspicious. Watch out for him. But above all, not a peep to anybody, not even God Himself. You understand, right?"

"Of course I understand," I answered as we shook hands. Andrei had a strong grip; he hurt my knuckles.

"Oh, yes, one more thing. Now that you can walk again I suggest that when you ride the train you try to mix with different people all the time, so that we don't attract attention as a group. We think that there are informers among us. I'll talk to you only when I have something to tell you. Otherwise, act like a stranger and keep your ears tuned in." Andrei got up and walked toward the latrine.

I was overwhelmed. The whole thing seemed unreal. Suppose Andrei himself was an informer. Was it safe to continue oversupplying rations? Was it possible for a starved band of prisoners to organize a conspiracy inside a Nazi camp right under their noses? I had never heard of one, but then, if it was a conspiracy, how could anybody hear of it? I had doubts about some of the things Andrei had told me; still, I decided to go along with it. I knew that life in camps wasn't worth very much, but here in Gusen Andrei at least offered me a chance to fight back.

I had not even had a chance to thank Andrei for healing my ankle; every time I had started to open my mouth he had launched into a new sentence.

It felt good to sit outside in the warm sun. Spring was beginning, but the air was still cool. Some birds flew overhead, too far away for me to tell what they were. They never came close to the camp, as if they sensed what went on there.

I started daydreaming about Alexandra. I saw her knocking at the studio window during the snowstorm, and I saw her throwing me a kiss the last time we had met. I remembered her having brought me the sweater, and how she had cried. It was all just a little over a year before, and yet it felt as though a whole lifetime had gone by.

I wondered if Alexandra still thought of me, if she remembered me at all, and I hoped she hadn't been caught with any of the pictures I had passed on to her. Maybe it wasn't a good idea to think of her, but how could I not? Perhaps I should only concentrate on what was happening at Gusen and stop worrying about things I couldn't help. That made more sense. Hadn't Andrei said that one day when all this was over he intended to go home because his family would be waiting for him? I couldn't be sure if anybody would be waiting for me, and I dreaded even thinking about it. The deportation night was constantly on my mind, and nightmarish images from the ghetto kept flooding back.

Prisoners were moving about aimlessly all around me, dragging their feet, exposing their emaciated bodies to the sun. Others stretched out on the bare ground, too tired and starved to move. It made me shudder when I realized that in a matter of days I could be one of those lifeless ones. What could one do? Sit back and wait for the end? At that moment I was more than ever convinced by Andrei.

My friend Michael came by and joined me. I couldn't talk to him about Andrei, but I told him about the Allied invasion of Normandy, something I had mentioned to no one except Andrei. He didn't want to believe me. I swore to him that I had read it in a Nazi paper clipping that, unfortunately, had by now disintegrated inside my shoe.

"I don't want to sound like a cynic," he said, "but I think somebody is lying."

"Would a Nazi-controlled paper boast about an Allied invasion?" I asked Michael. "Usually they would underreport on Allied progress or not mention it at all. Can't you see?" I insisted.

I couldn't convince him, so I gave up. He didn't feel well, he told me. He was losing strength. I tried to instill some hope in him, even if the invasion was a newspaper lie. Michael and I had known each other since before the war. We were of the same age, had traveled together from one camp to another, and had sometimes even landed in the same barracks. I was sorry he didn't know how to dream.

In spite of the Messerschmitt food supplements people were still dying of malnutrition. Somehow, however, the core of the plant force kept functioning. Two Russian friends out of my food commando of five had died and were never replaced. Now the three of us were carrying a heavier load. In addition, we had been assigned the chore of boiling fifty quarts of skimmed milk in a field kitchen twice a week for the prisoners who were spraying the airplane fuselages at the plant. It was ironic that the Nazis were so concerned with the lungs of a few paint sprayers while they let others die by the thousands. Nothing they did made any sense.

April arrived, and with it came new hope. One day we were ordered to dig air-raid shelters outside the camp perimeter, and soon, sure enough, Allied planes arrived, bombing some locations in the vicinity. Although we were their targets we welcomed their bombs with open arms and no reservations. We didn't mind dying for freedom, and in order to end such evil. I prayed for the planes to return and bomb the Nazis again and again. I loved to watch the SS men with their automatic rifles run for their lives at the first sound of the camp siren. Suddenly they didn't look so tough at all. Andrei was right when he had said that we would win, because in our hearts we believed that we were free men. I knew what he meant. I could feel it when he said that our ideas would survive but the Nazi evil wouldn't. There was something magic in his words. Even though I didn't understand everything he said, I was willing to fight with him.

Around the middle of April, even as bombs were falling, an accident took place at the plant's loading ramp. As a freight train filled with Messerschmitt fuselages left the loading ramp a prisoner fell onto the tracks and was cut in half by the wheels. The man turned out to be the Czech about whom Andrei had warned me. I wondered who had contrived the accident. It had to be one of Andrei's men, I thought; I only hoped that the Nazis wouldn't take revenge.

An investigation followed, and the Gestapo were brought in. They brought dogs and led an interrogation, but nothing came of it. They questioned the German engineer of the train and everyone else who was in the vicinity when the accident occurred. The mere fact that they brought in the Gestapo was an indication that the Czech had been important to the Nazis. Andrei had been right. Normally they would hardly have noticed the death of a prisoner; this was what we were there for.

That same day one of Andrei's men was searched by the SS while returning from the plant to camp. They found on him a piece of metal resembling a trigger assembly component and took him in for questioning. They broke his ribs, knocked out his teeth, and shipped him half-dead to the crematorium in Mauthausen. He didn't talk, I found out later. If he had, almost certainly he would have lived.

The following morning I saw Andrei on the train. "Don't cut any extra bread," he said to me quietly, "until the excitement dies down. It's very easy to do something foolish, and this is what they're looking for."

Things were getting worse for the Nazis, as well as for us, day by day. There was a shortage of metals and tools at the plant; most of the machines were now idle. In lieu of our usual work we were ordered to sweep the plant or polish and oil the machines. Even grease was in short supply. Our bread rations were cut, the Messerschmitt food supplement was eliminated altogether, and no more German soup of bones, beans, and cabbage appeared.

Early one morning when we were on our way to the plant Allied planes flew over again, but they didn't drop any bombs. We were all sorry. We were ordered to abandon the train and lie on our backs in the field. Watching the sky, I thought I would have given my right arm to be up there so that I could bomb that miserable rat hole to dust. I could see little dark clouds exploding in the sky and kept praying for the Nazis to miss their targets. It was all over within a few minutes.

Soon artillery rumblings and bomb explosions became commonplace, and the whole camp trembled. We no longer went to the plant, but we also found food to be scarcer and scarcer. During the night of May third, 1945, the SS command disappeared from the camp, leaving behind a skeleton crew of lesser rank, and a Red Cross flag was hoisted on top of a tall mast in the center of the camp. Armed with vintage rifles, Austrian Home Guards, veterans of World War I, were brought in to guard us. They were in their fifties and wore vintage uniforms sizes too large for them. The watchtowers were still manned by SS men armed with machine guns, however.

The following day, May fourth, there was no bread. We were ordered to stay in the barracks and not to congregate outside. Dimitri came over to my bunk and sat down next to me. Almost in a whisper he said, "Tomorrow at midnight something will happen. Don't take off your shoes when you go to sleep. That's all," and he moved on.

The rest of the day was uneventful. Around midday two containers of watery soup were brought in to our barrack, not enough for three hundred people; that was all we ate that day. That morning I ate the bit of bread I had saved from my last breakfast and cleaned my pocket of every crumb; I was still hungry. My friend Ilya came over to tell me that the German *kapos* had received Red Cross parcels and were having a real party. He suspected that the parcels were meant for us, the prisoners, and not the *kapos.* Also, two prisoners were shot by an SS guard who caught them engaging in cannibalism. "Has it gotten this bad?" I asked. "Yes," Ilya said. "It could get even worse if this continues much longer." Ilya made a few comments about Andrei being a courageous man. I wasn't sure why he did so, but I carefully avoided getting involved in a discussion about Andrei. Suppose Ilya wasn't a member of the conspiracy; even if he were, he wasn't supposed to talk about others who were. I pretended not to understand his references, though I had a funny feeling that Ilya was trying to tell me something. Confused, I decided to rest in my bunk. That way I would be ready when midnight arrived. Soon I was fast asleep, dreaming what the camp takeover would look like.

Suddenly I heard rifle shots and small explosions. Then a voice in Russian came over a bullhorn warning us to stay inside. There were more rifle shots and the sporadic rattling of a machine gun or two. Somebody yelled that Block #4 was on fire.

When the shooting stopped I ventured outside. All the watchtowers were burning, and some SS guards were on the ground, flat on their backs. Andrei appeared holding an automatic, still pointing it at a burning tower, with several hand grenades dangling from his belt. He wore a German helmet, which made him look very odd. There must have been more than a hundred armed Russian prisoners sweeping the camp grounds. They moved in small groups, crouching and surveying the ground.

The Austrian Home Guards were the first to be overpowered and disarmed; their rifles were used against the guards in the towers. The Home Guards had been taken prisoner inside one of the barracks. Nobody tried to harm them; they were for the most part old and harmless. The SS guards took off from their compound, leaving most of their heavy weapons and lots of canned food. There were about thirty of them, mostly Lithuanians and Ukrainians. At first they attempted to resist, but quickly they changed their minds.

The electricians of the conspiracy succeeded in cutting the power lines and telephone lines; later they secured an opening into the guardhouse. As I watched the camp gate being barricaded somebody called my name. I turned and saw Dimitri with a group of others rushing toward the main gate. "Come along," he yelled out, "we need help." I ran as fast as I could.

Andrei feared that the SS might decide to come back to take revenge; he thought it would be wise to fortify the gate. So we brought down a machine gun and several cases of ammunition and set up at the gate, lining up a long row of gasoline bombs against the fence. Other machine-gun nests were set up at various points; we filled potato sacks with earth and stacked them around the guns.

The place was beginning to look like an armed camp, although not everybody had a gun. By now hundreds of Russians were engaged in fortifying the camp; whoever was still able to walk lent a hand. Captured food was brought to the camp kitchen where prisoner-cooks busily prepared our first soup in days. A group of armed prisoners left for the nearby farms and returned with a wagon loaded with food-stuffs. Everyone seemed to know what had to be done.

Andrei was the undisputed leader. He shouted commands to his lieutenants, who in turn passed them on down the ranks. So this was what he had been talking about.

I felt someone pulling at my sleeve; my next-bunk neighbor decided to wake me because I was yelling and making all kinds of sounds in my sleep. "Were you fighting a war?" he asked. "I guess I was dreaming. Don't mind me," I said apologetically.

The liberation scenes were still vivid in my mind when the morning lineup was called. The old Austrian guards were still everywhere, even in the towers. Was it possible that the SS guards had left? Was my dream real, or was I still dreaming?

It must have been early afternoon when suddenly we heard voices coming from the compound yelling *"Amerykance, Amerykance."* Three American reconnaissance tanks with white stars painted on them rumbled along a nearby road on their way to Linz. I ran outside with the hundreds of others who could still run. I was overwhelmed. I know I was screaming, but I don't know what it was I was saying. Two tanks stopped at the gate with their engines running, their steel bulks covered with dried mud. Helmeted soldiers with smiling faces appeared in the gun turrets, their eyes covered with goggles. I tried to remember the few words of English I knew, but I didn't think they were appropriate. I addressed the soldiers in French. When one of them asked "Who are you?" I didn't know what to say, however; I wasn't sure who I really was. *"Liberté,"* I yelled, not being able to think of anything else. The soldier just smiled and waved at me. Does this mean I'm free? I wondered as I ripped the cloth tag with my number—#88415, will I ever forget it?—off my jacket.

It would be impossible to describe the exhilaration that several thousand starved, sick, and exhausted people were able to generate when only two hours earlier they would not have dreamed that such an event was possible. Prisoners riddled with typhus and fever, prisoners who had not walked in days, rose from their bunks and crawled to see the tanks for themselves. Everyone was laughing and crying at once. We wanted to kiss the tanks, if we could only get close enough.

The Americans had not known that we—or the camp—existed. They had to move on, they told us, toward Linz; they assured us, however, that the war was almost over, would be in a day or two at most. Some hours later Red Cross ambulances arrived with Allied medical personnel, and the camp was turned into a field hospital.

Soon a strong odor of disinfectant permeated the place; everything seemed to be saturated with it. Inside the barracks long lines of sick prisoners, naked to the waist, their rib cages hollow-looking, stood patiently waiting to be examined by doctors. I walked away from the lineup; I wanted to get as far away from death as I possibly could. I couldn't stand being in Gusen another minute. Through the open window of the sick bay I saw piles of corpses, some with their eyes still open.

Before leaving I went to look for Andrei to say good-bye. I walked through the camp asking people if they had seen him, but no one could say for certain that they had, and some didn't even know what he looked like. With a heavy heart I walked alone through the gate. Outside I linked up with four friends; starved as we were, we set out on the road to Linz. Spring was in full swing; the warm air was invigorating, and the bright colors were nearly blinding. I was able to breathe at last. I couldn't believe I was free again.

AN ENCOUNTER
IN LINZ

On May 6, 1945, twenty-four hours after I was liberated from Gusen, I was exploring the streets of the very foreign-feeling city of Linz. As I had walked out of that hell I had promised myself to forget everything I remembered; later I found it difficult to believe that I was even alive. I wanted a new identity and a new lease on life; I felt at a loss, totally detached from everything I had once known. Faint images and strange faces moved before my eyes. I could make no sense of them and simply kept moving. After hours of walking I wound up in a residential area; everywhere I looked I saw small, well-kept homes with fenced-in gardens. Hardly anyone was in sight. An elderly couple walked by, their eyes focused intently on the sidewalk, as if they were looking for something they had lost. I felt as if I had known this neighborhood, that just around the corner would be a house I recognized, but every time I turned a corner everything was the same, strange and foreign. It was so peaceful I felt as if I were in a dream, that all this wasn't real.

The sun shone brilliantly; the sky was dotted with small, puffy clouds. Around the next corner I saw an elderly couple sitting side by side in worn armchairs on the front porch of their house. They could have been my grandparents vacationing, they could have been any old couple in my home town. I walked over to the fence and—for some reason—stopped. Much to my surprise, the couple greeted me and invited me to join them on the porch, which I did.

The man rose and introduced himself. "Herr Gartner and Frau Gartner, my wife," he said, pointing at the woman sitting next to him. He pulled over a heavy metal garden chair and asked me to sit down. Herr Gartner was a bit on the pudgy side and had a round, unshaven face with several days' growth of stubble. He wore a gray felt hat turning to green around the band, a pair of faded corduroy pants, a green cardigan sweater worn at the elbows, and a pair of felt slippers. The sour smell of perspiration emanated from him. Frau Gartner was thin and bony, almost sickly-looking. She had dark eyes with long lashes and held her hands clasped as if in prayer. She wore an old flowery housedress with a dark woolen blazer over it; she had wound a scarf around her neck. Before I had a chance to introduce myself Frau Gartner spoke up. "Please have some tea with us," she said in a low voice.

"Thank you very much, I hope I am not imposing," I responded, stunned by the invitation.

"No, not at all," she assured me. "It will be nice to have someone to talk to. My husband and I have been alone for quite some time." She stood up and went into the house; soon she returned carrying a tray with three cups of tea and a basket of cookies.

I quickly introduced myself and told the Gartners about my time in the camps. Herr Gartner told me the public had been assured that such camps were only for criminals, communists, and antistate elements, but they hadn't believed it. I assured him that my only crime was that I happened to be Jewish. The Gartners were understanding and very apologetic. Herr Gartner told me that he was a friend of the Jews; during World War I he was stationed in Poland with the Austrian Imperial Army, and he had become friendly with a number of Jewish families. He was very fond of Jews, he said. He and his wife had also suffered a loss, he recalled sadly, since two of their sons and a nephew who had served in the Wehrmacht never came back from the war.

Frau Gartner urged me to eat. I didn't have to be asked twice; I hadn't tasted a cookie since I was in Maidanek with Leon, a little over a year before. I was hungry, but I tried to control my appetite. I didn't want them to know how starved I really was. We sat on the porch talking for a long time; before I knew it, it was past curfew. Herr Gartner said I couldn't walk back to the city and suggested that I spend the night. The Gartners had ample room; there was an empty bedroom on the second floor that hadn't been used for some time. It had belonged to Horst, one of their sons who hadn't come back from the war. I was asked to make myself at home. I was very grateful for their hospitality and immediately got to like the Gartners.

Frau Gartner served a vegetable broth with beans and potatoes; it was the best meal I had tasted in a long time. I washed it down with ersatz coffee and felt better than I had in ages. Frau Gartner told me at length about how difficult the war had been and how happy they were that it was finally over. Everything had been rationed, and there had been long lines in front of shops. I heard her out, marveling over how little the Gartners knew about what had happened to us in Poland and in the rest of Nazi-occupied Europe. I decided not to get into this. I thanked Frau Gartner for her good supper, and her husband showed me upstairs to my room.

The smallish room was square in shape and furnished with antiques. It had an old mahogany bed with a tall bedstead; next to it stood a night table. Across the room was a matching chest of drawers. At the foot of the bed stood an old trunk adorned with lots of metal. The floor was covered with a bright Oriental rug. Herr Gartner showed me to the bathroom and made sure that I had everything I needed; he then turned on the lamp on the night table and left.

The first thing I noticed after Herr Gartner had gone was

the mirror on the wall; I had not seen myself since before the camps. Reflected was the face of a perfect stranger—gaunt, gray, wholly unfamiliar. I was shocked. I tried to smile and do imitations; pulling my lower lip down over my chin, I made myself into my uncle in Warsaw. I found a pair of old glasses in the bathroom and tried them on; my magnified eyes reminded me of my grandfather. I stood in front of the mirror making faces until I ran out of characters to imitate and finally gave up. This was how I remembered my relatives. They became real; the mirror brought them back.

Next I noticed something I had not seen before because of my fascination with the mirror. On the wall hung a framed certificate of achievement from the Hitler Youth. Next to it was another certificate issued in the name of Horst Gartner, congratulating him upon his acceptance into the Waffen SS. Between and above the two certificates hung a picture of a young man in a black uniform with skull-and-crossbones insignia in his lapels and on his cap. I stood there, a cold sweat running down my back, studying the photograph. The young man's sunken eyes reminded me of the skull insignia on his cap and lapels; they were equally expressionless. On his left cheek below his eye was a scar.

Didn't his parents know what the SS was about? Why did Herr Gartner tell me that his sons had served in the Wehrmacht? I kept thinking, How ignorant does he think I am? And I have to sleep in this murderer's bed? There wasn't much I could do about it. The curfew was on, confining me to the house; I decided to go to bed.

As I was about to stretch out, on impulse I pulled out the night table drawer and saw a packet of mail inside it tied with a worn white ribbon. There were several letters from a Scharenführer Horst Gartner of the Einsatzkommando with the return address of Feld Post at the Ostfront. That was in Russia. They dated back to 1942 and 1943. Unable to resist, I pulled out one letter. I knew what the Einsatzkommando was all about; they were the butchers and the killers in Europe. I unfolded the letter and with difficulty began to decode Horst Gartner's not very neat Gothic handwriting. I always had difficulties reading the Gothic alphabet.

Horst Gartner told his parents how proud he was to be a part of this modern crusade and how honorably he was serving the Reich and the New Order of Europe. He hoped that they were proud of him, too. I nearly fainted. How could Herr Gartner pretend not to know any of this about his own son? I couldn't believe it. He must have known what the SS was about; he couldn't be that gullible. Such a sweet, hospitable couple. I was shaking with rage. I deposited the letters in the drawer and went to bed; I was too exhausted to stay up any longer. As I was about to fall asleep a thought occurred to me. Suppose their son Horst was back here in hiding? He might come at any moment to his parents' house: it was a possibility. What then? I decided to try not to fall asleep. I dozed off but woke up several times, disturbed by someone's snoring. Later on it got quiet again; I could hear an insect buzzing at the window. I was a nervous wreck. The slightest sound made me jump. I imagined all kinds of things; I couldn't forgive myself for having been so truthful. Finally it started to get light. I looked out the window to see the rising sun and decided to leave the Gartners as soon as I possibly could.

Suddenly I heard a gentle knocking at my door. I went over to open it, and there was Herr Gartner, entirely dressed, excusing himself for waking me up. It was not quite seven o'clock, and he and his wife were going out to get in the breadline, he told me. They would be back within the hour, he hoped. He just wanted to let me know that I would be left in the house alone; would I mind? I assured him that it would be all right. "I'm a big fellow," I remember having said. As soon as they left I washed up and prepared to leave. I watched them through the window to make sure that the two of them had gone; I didn't think I could face them again after the discoveries of the evening. I was sorry to leave so rudely, but I had no alternative; to me they were part of a conspiracy, parents of a murderer. I found a pencil and some paper on the kitchen table and decided to write them a thank-you note. I concocted a lie about a toothache, saying I had to find a dentist in a hurry; I excused myself for leaving without saying good-bye in person and thanked them for their hospitality. I never gave them the slightest hint that I knew anything about their son.

Somewhere in the house a clock struck nine times. It sounded like the clock in my grandparents' house. I looked into the next room and saw a silver candle holder—exactly the kind of a candle holder I used to see every Friday night on our dining room table—atop a dresser. There was no doubt in my mind that it had come from a Jewish home. It had a massive square base and was etched with a pattern of grape leaves. Obviously it was part of a pair. Why only one? I kept wondering. As I turned to leave I saw a little alcove with a small mahogany table inside it; on top of the table was the other candle holder. Next to it stood a silver Passover wine cup with the Star of David engraved on it. I was incensed. Herr Gartner must have known that these were items of Jewish origin. How could he pretend to such ignorance? It was unforgivable.

A gray and white cat on the porch watched me leave. He tried to come closer, but I chased him away. I made sure to memorize the address.

It was still chilly outside, but the air was invigorating. I wasn't sure which streets to take back to the city and started out rather blindly, hoping not to bump into my hosts. I stopped a youngster and asked him for directions. As it turned out, I was on the right track, and soon enough I was back in Linz. The city was alive with people. Groups of liberated prisoners of various nationalities congregated at street corners and in the squares, trying to communicate with American soldiers. Most of them were still dressed in their striped camp uniforms; some wore civilian clothes they must have found in abandoned homes or had received from charities. None of the garments fit by a long shot. Emaciated faces attempted smiles, creating deep lines around the former prisoners' cheeks. All sorts of questions were being asked in every imaginable tongue.

Austrian women rushed by with little children in strollers, overloaded with personal belongings. There were few young men to be seen. Most of the shops were still barricaded; others had been broken into and were totally empty. Only bakeries were open; long lines of elderly people formed in front of them, waiting for their bread rations. Everything was being rationed, even milk. The Austrians seemed to be used to this system, and they waited patiently, with blank expressions on their faces, for their turn. None of them smiled or spoke. I felt sorry for them and hated them at the same time. These were the parents of our killers and executioners. Didn't they know what had happened to most of Europe? How could they not have known what their sons and husbands had been up to?

I continued on aimlessly, thinking about the Gartners. I imagined Horst everywhere, watching me, following me, waiting for the right moment to kill me. I was almost sure I had seen his face before, perhaps in one of the camps, in transit, or maybe in the ghetto. I couldn't be certain any longer, but I knew those eyes I had seen in the photograph: eyes that sized up the victim while they waited for the kill. I was getting paranoid and hungry; I was obsessed with the idea that Horst was after me. I decided to get out of Linz.

Two years later, after I had emigrated to America, I wrote to the Gartners. I still remembered their address. Almost immediately I received an answer. Herr Gartner informed me that Frau Gartner had died. Evidently she had suffered a heart attack when she had found out that their son Horst was tried by a Polish court and subsequently executed. Herr Gartner didn't elaborate about Horst's trial or about his crimes. He himself had diabetes and said he would be very grateful if I could mail some insulin to him, as there was a shortage of it in Austria. He also told me that of the six Gartner relatives who had fought in the German army a single nephew had come back. He was a paraplegic, confined to a wheelchair. War wasn't good for anybody, he concluded, not even for the people at the top who started it.

I sent insulin regularly for some time until one day I received a letter from his nephew announcing that Herr Gartner had died. In his will he had left me a silver wine cup and two silver candlesticks.

REUNIONS

It was May, 1945, and the war was over. For two days I had been in Linz, Austria, alone, living in constant anxiety over the fate of my family. I was afraid to think about who was still alive. Every day I crisscrossed the city of Linz, hoping to find a trace of something familiar, a clue, a contact of some kind. I wasn't even sure if I still remembered the faces of my brother and sister or my parents; I wasn't sure that they would recognize me if we were to meet.

Nightmarish images were always before my eyes, keeping me awake at night. I had nothing left, not even a picture, to prove that I had once belonged to a family. I didn't know who I was; I had doubts about my own name. I remembered only my prisoner number, as if it were engraved on my brain.

Who am I, I kept asking myself, and what am I doing here? I looked and searched but kept running away from myself.

Soon I moved on to Salzburg, about seventy-five miles from Linz, to get away from an imaginary SS man I thought was out to kill me. In my mind he looked like Horst Gartner, whose parents had invited me to stay at their house. Salzburg was no better, only somewhat larger than Linz; registrations and inquiries, survivors looking for relatives, lists of survivors on walls, and notices in different languages were everywhere. Everybody was looking for somebody else, but no one, it seemed, was looking for me. I found no familiar names, not even that of a neighbor. Slowly I was coming to terms with the fact that, at the age of twenty, I was alone in the world.

One early morning, while walking near the railway station in search of a photo shop, I heard someone calling from the other side of the street. The call came again; it was my name. At first I couldn't identify with it; when I finally turned I saw a stocky young man of medium height with a full, round face and closely cropped hair. Who was he? He had the face of a stranger, and his voice was unfamiliar. He was wearing a pair of baggy pants and a striped shirt with rolled-up sleeves; he carried a small suitcase with reinforced metal corners.

When I stopped he started running toward me, yelling my name at the top of his lungs. When he realized I wasn't responding he dropped the suitcase, grabbed me by my shoulders, and shook me hard, as if trying to wake me from a sleep.

"I'm your brother, don't you recognize me?" he yelled. He had heard that I was in Austria and had traveled for two days from Stuttgart, sitting on top of a coal car, to look for me. "Are you all right?" he asked. "Or is there something wrong with you?" We hugged, and he nearly squashed me; he was strong.

"I just couldn't recognize you," I said, fighting back my tears. "I didn't think I would ever see you again. It's almost unreal how different you look; you've gained a lot of weight, your hair is short. God, you look like a different person. How could I have recognized you?"

"I had a bad case of typhoid," he said, "and since I got well I haven't been able to stop eating. I've been liberated since April and have been living on a farm with some friends. Recently we slaughtered a pig; you can imagine how well we eat.

"You probably don't know that Father was shot," my brother went on to say. He had witnessed Father's execution. Matter-of-factly he described the whole scene to me. "I begged the SS man to let Father go," he told me, "but he threatened to shoot me, too, and I think he would have if I hadn't stepped back into the ranks. I remember him very well. I even know his name and where he came from. It was terrible and frightening. I can't forget it."

For a split second I remembered my father throwing the egg to me at the Szkolna camp. I remembered his tears when the SS guard hit him with a stick for doing so; every time I thought of my father there were tears; still, I couldn't cry. It seemed impossible that I was talking to my brother.

An Austrian woman with big, sad eyes and a knapsack strapped to her back stopped to watch us; she stood a few feet away shaking her head. I didn't think she knew what was happening or who we were, but when we started walking away she looked back over her shoulder, still shaking her head. I heard her say *"Wie traurig"*—how sad—before we disappeared around the corner.

My brother had heard rumors from survivors who traveled across Europe looking for their families that our sister Hanka was alive and looking for us in Poland.

We stayed together for a while, but toward the end of the summer we parted again. My brother remained in Germany; I went to Poland via Prague to search for our sister.

It was a difficult and lonely journey that took me back to a country I dreaded, a journey full of strange and unpredictable encounters. I traveled in the backs of trucks or in unheated trains, standing up for hours on steps or in open freight cars, often enough in the rain. The Nazis had robbed the country of everything; there were few scheduled trains or buses. The same hateful faces greeted me wherever I went. The same resentment came through all of their eyes; I could see they were wondering why I had come back.

Cold winds and rain blew incessantly across the Polish landscape, turning it into one huge mud pie. I traveled from one city to another searching for my sister, only to find that she had eluded me each time by leaving a day or two before I arrived. I kept moving from place to place, hoping to catch up with her; in Lodz a Polish friend of the family, Mr. S., gave me some money my parents had left with him for safekeeping and told me that my sister had left for Stettin on her way to the west.

The following day I hitched a ride on a truck going toward the German frontier. As soon as I climbed in the back of the truck it started raining, so I slipped under the tarpaulin and stretched out on a pile of potato sacks behind some wooden crates. It was late in the evening when the truck approached the first intersection; it slowed down. I heard part of a conversation with the driver, and soon I saw two armed men in uniforms climb in the back. They settled themselves directly across from where I was lying; even in the dark something told me that they weren't friendly.

I was correct in my assessment; when the truck started moving again I heard the two men talking. They complained about what a wasted day it had been; they hadn't found a single Jew. I broke out in a cold sweat. What if they discovered me? Suppose they decided to lift the tarpaulin. That would be the end of me. What could I possibly tell them? About my time in the camps, and how much I longed to get back to my home town and find my people? How could they understand me if they were out to kill me? Only several days before I had heard someone talk about armed bands of Polish nationalists who were organizing pogroms against Jewish survivors. These people were no better than the Nazis; I hated the thought that I might have survived the camps to meet my fate at the hands of Polish hooligans.

My stomach felt as if it were tied into a knot. I tried not to move or even breathe. If only I could shrink to the size of an insect or change into an earthworm! Kafka's *Metamorphosis* came to my mind, and I prayed for a miracle.

Suddenly I felt like sneezing. I was terrified; instinctively I pressed my nose against the edge of a crate and stopped breathing. It worked. I hoped I wouldn't have to repeat the trick; next time I might not be as lucky. I could still hear my traveling companions making threats against the Jews.

It must have been well past midnight. There was no moon, and the rain was coming down incessantly. One side of my face kept getting wet, and drops of water were rolling down my neck behind my shirt collar. It was getting cold; I began to shiver. From time to time the truck would zigzag to avoid a pothole, and the smaller load at the tail of the truck would slide and bounce against the crates, pushing them against my legs.

The two men continued to discuss their exploits and their frustrations. The one with the hoarser voice was recounting how he and some of his friends had recently executed a whole Jewish family who had survived the war in an underground shelter in the woods. He described the episode in vivid detail. It was a bloodcurdling story. The two men sat at the edge of the truck with their feet hanging down and with their backs to me. With one eye I was able to make out their silhouetted torsos against the misty night.

Some hours passed, and finally I heard a knocking above my head, at the driver's cab window. At the next intersection the truck came to a stop, and the two men got off. I watched them jump across the ditch and disappear into the woods. I felt as though I had been liberated for the second time.

I didn't know how far it was to Stettin, but I didn't care. I crawled from under the tarpaulin and looked out. It had stopped raining, and the haze was lifting. There was a strong aroma of rotting leaves mixed with cow manure. At the side of the road I could see faint outlines of bare trees with twisted branches, as if multitudes of crisscrossing arms were reaching for the sky. Some distance away I could make out farm huts with thatched roofs; the flickering lights of kerosene lamps reflected against their tiny windows, making them look like squatting monsters with burning eyes.

It was a sad and desolate landscape. Here and there were clusters of birch and pine trees. The white birch trunks seemed to be moving across the fields like ghosts, as though they were racing with the truck. From time to time I could hear the driver curse in Polish or sing old Jewish tunes. I was astounded. How did he know Jewish tunes? He had a husky voice and a rich vocabulary of four-letter words with which he seemed to amuse himself.

It was dawn when the truck reached the gates of the city. When it came to a full stop the driver clambered out of the cab, yawning and stretching, to announce our arrival in the city of Stettin. This was as far as he was going.

"This is it," he said. "Last stop." I jumped off the truck holding on to my knapsack. Every muscle in my body ached. I walked over to the driver. He was a husky blond man, perhaps in his thirties. "How do you happen to know Jewish tunes?" I asked him carefully.

"Oh, well," he answered, "it's a long story, but since you ask I'll tell you. I happen to be Jewish. Simple as that. So are you, right? I didn't even have a good look at you, but my antennae tell me you must be one, too," he said, winking at me.

"How could I deny it?" I asked him, and the two of us laughed. It felt so much safer now that the trip was over.

"By the way," I said, "do you happen to know who those two armed men were you had on your truck?"

"I don't know them personally, but I imagine they were members of some political faction; fanatics. There are quite a few of them around, and they always hitch rides; it could be dangerous for me to refuse them. Don't forget, they're armed, and I'm not."

"I was frightened when they got on the truck," I admitted. "They were really dangerous."

"Frankly, I had no idea you were Jewish," he said. "I never had a good look at you before you got on the truck. But don't be afraid, it's over. God protected you."

"You look so Polish, so Christian," I said. "I would have never taken you for a Jew."

"That is exactly what saved me," he said. "My looks. But who are you, and where are you going?" he asked. I told him briefly where I came from and for whom I was looking. "My God," he exclaimed, "it must have been real tough for you. You should be happy to be alive and have a sister. Look at me; I'm the only one from my family left alive. I know what it is like to be left alone."

When I tried to reward him for his trouble he wouldn't accept any money. I offered him my last pack of Chesterfields, but he would only take a few cigarettes. He drove me closer to the center of the city and let me off in front of a teahouse surrounded by ruins. "This is the only place in Stettin where you can get some food. Good luck. I hope you find her," he said, smiling and shaking my hand.

I was in a strange city in which only a few buildings remained standing. It was still early. The teahouse was open, however; I could smell freshly baked bread, and the aroma reminded me of my hunger. I hadn't eaten since I got on the truck in Lodz almost twelve hours before. In the teahouse marble tables stood on massive wrought-iron stands; a long marble counter adorned with brass fixtures, a reminder of better times, ran the length of the room. On the wall hung a small Polish flag.

A young woman was filling orders behind the counter, and a teenager with a blond ponytail was waiting on tables. They didn't have much to offer; only hot tea and buttered rolls or bread. For me that fare was a treat. I sat there warming my hands on a tall glass full of steaming tea, feeling the warmth travel all the way down to my frozen toes. The place began to fill up. People were drifting in, settling in at the tables, dragging metal chairs noisily over the marble floor. I noticed a young man enter the teahouse. He wore a creased raincoat tied with a wide leather belt and carried a knapsack. He looked around as if searching for someone, then proceeded directly toward my table, where there was an empty chair. "Is it all right if I join you?" he asked.

"Please do; I haven't talked to a soul in days," I answered.

"My name is Moshe, Moshe Feingold. I'm a survivor," he

introduced himself, shaking my hand rather vigorously. He pulled out the chair across from me and quickly sat down, dropping his knapsack under the table next to mine. I told him my name, and he leaned forward, coming closer to me, as if he had difficulty hearing.

"I think you must be a survivor," Moshe said in a low voice, looking at me suspiciously. "Yes, I am," I answered. "Now that our hair is still short, our clothing fits badly, and we look hungry, lost, and frightened, it must be easy to tell," I said.

"You're quite right," Moshe said, biting into his buttered roll. He was thin, and his eyes were dark and intense. When he talked his head kept turning like a radar dish, left to right, right to left. His short, curly hair was growing in in a very odd shape; the curls were connecting and pressing on each other, as if fighting for space. We sat there exchanging stories, ordering more and more tea. As far as he knew, his entire family had disappeared.

"I crisscrossed Poland, I went to see every camp that ever existed, and all I found were piles of ashes. Poland is one huge cemetery. What else is left?" he asked. "I come from Otwock, not far from Warsaw. There is not a single Jew left in the town. I got married one week before the war started. I had a wife and a little son. My son would have been four years old by now. My parents, my wife's parents, and the rest of the family were shipped to Treblinka. This much I found out."

I felt bad for him and didn't think it was appropriate for me to talk about my losses. Moshe was on his way to the west, he told me, to join some friends who were getting ready to emigrate to Palestine. We wished each other luck; a few hours into the morning he left.

I got up and went over to the counter to buy some more rolls, but before I had a chance to place my order the young woman behind the counter asked me excitedly, "Do you happen to have a relative named Hanka? I don't know her last name. You look just like her, the same mouth and eyes, the same face. She's my neighbor. She lives right around the corner, on the second floor to the right. I know her. She usually comes here for her rolls. I'm surprised she didn't show up yet this morning. I noticed the strong resemblance as soon as you came in, but then I got busy, and I lost track of you."

"I'm her brother," I answered, my knees shaking. "I've been looking for her everywhere for weeks."

"Please sit down and have some more tea," she suggested. "You must be starved. All this traveling in such bad weather." I thanked her and told her I had already eaten well, paid my check, and ran outside.

It was still early when I knocked at my sister's apartment. A young woman dressed in a long robe opened the door and instantly threw her arms around me.

"How did you find me? This is a miracle. I've been looking for you all over Poland," I heard her say into my shoulder. I couldn't speak. There were no tears, only sadness, and when we hugged a strange feeling came over me. It was as if something inside me was asking me why I was alive while so many others weren't. It pressed and nagged at me, bringing back images of those who were gone. Should I tell my sister immediately what had happened to our father? Or should I wait? I had a feeling that she already knew, that she, too, must have been wondering if I knew about Father.

I wanted to tell my sister how happy I was to find her, but I couldn't find the words. It all seemed abstract, hardly believable. What was one supposed to talk about at such moments? There was no point in recalling the tragic events; it was simply good to be alive, and to be together. Over the next few days we talked at length about many different things but never mentioned the war, nor the camps, as if it had never taken place, as if the six years had just dropped out of the calendar and disappeared. I was getting used to the idea that I was free, no longer alone, and that there were others like myself, roaming, searching, and wandering.

About ten days after my arrival my sister left Stettin, heading for the west to join our brother, and I set out in search of Alexandra, my wartime underground contact. I planned to rejoin my family as soon as I found her.

ON MEMORY

In April of 1983, two weeks after the magazine I worked for had published my photographs of and report on the Gathering of Holocaust Survivors in Washington, D.C., I received a telephone call from a well-spoken woman whom I had never met before. She spoke with a slight French accent and told me that she was married to a man who came from Radom, my home town in Poland, and that they lived in Switzerland. A few days earlier, on a flight from the Far East to Europe, they had come across a copy of the magazine that carried my article. Would it be possible, she asked, for her husband to meet me for lunch? Slightly puzzled, I agreed to a meeting; a few days later we met at a midtown Manhattan restaurant. The husband was an elegantly dressed man with a kind face, smiling blue eyes, and short-cropped, graying hair. His name was Selig. He spoke impeccable English.

We sat down at a table and made a toast. No formalities, no introductory ceremonies. It was almost as if we had known each other before. We acted like old friends who had not seen each other for a long time. There was a lot to talk about; we conversed in English, now and then switching to Polish. As it turned out, although we had both grown up in Radom, our paths had never crossed. Selig was somewhat younger than I. We did establish that we had had a mutual acquaintance who had since died. Did I know where he used to live in Radom? He could not remember the name of the street, but he knew what it was near. I named the street for him, and he was delighted. I also knew of the school he had attended. It was a prestigious private school for children from well-to-do families. I had gone to a public school; it was tuition-free and a haven for anti-Semitic hooligans.

"How could you stand it?" he asked.

"How could we stand the camps?" I countered.

"Oh, well, there was no choice."

"Yes, you're right, but why then didn't we create our own choices?"

"Because it wasn't up to us to do that," he said.

"Look at our history," I said. "Was it ever any different?"

I really wanted to know why he was there, what had prompted him to call on a stranger.

Finally, rather abruptly, he confessed. "You know, I survived the camps, but I lost everybody. After the war I moved to Switzerland, went to school, got married, raised a family, became successful in business. Years went by, and eventually I forgot about my experiences. I never spoke to anyone about them. I thought that finally I was able to leave the past behind me and to adjust happily to a new and productive life. That was true until two weeks ago, when I picked up the magazine with your article about the Washington Gathering. After I read it I realized that you're right, one cannot and must not forget."

I was speechless and deeply touched. His eyes were moist, and I knew that he was trying very hard not to cry.

Selig's presence reminded me of a very special childhood friend whom I hadn't seen since the end of the war. In 1945—thirty-eight years earlier, to be exact—I was a prisoner in Gusen II. The Nazis were in retreat, the end of the war was

171

in sight, but in Gusen II—totally isolated behind barbed-wire fences and guarded by well-armed SS men—we had no way of knowing as much.

Gusen II consisted of several thousand inmates, many of them Russian prisoners of war. The camp itself was located in the middle of a fertile valley twenty-five kilometers south of Linz and fifteen minutes by cattle train from St. Georgen, where Herr Messerschmitt had built an airplane factory in order to keep the inmates of Gusen II occupied. The factory, which consisted of a maze of interconnected underground tunnels, was built at the expense of thirty thousand Russian prisoners' lives, I was told. The factory was nearly finished when I arrived late in the summer of 1944. In my transport, among others, was my childhood friend Michael.

One day in the fall Michael and I made friends with a Russian prisoner about ten years our senior named Ilya. He had been a paramedic in the Russian army and knew a lot about first aid. We all worked the same shift and many times traveled together to the factory by train. Michael and I became very fond of Ilya, and he responded in kind. We helped one another in every possible way. We thought that Ilya was an honorable man and could be trusted. We talked about our dilemma, about the war and our childhoods, and we realized that we had a lot in common: We valued life.

On Sundays we would sit outdoors with our backs to the barrack, greeting the first rays of the spring sun. Ilya would recite poetry by Pushkin. The verse sounded beautiful, even though I couldn't understand most of it. It was like music, something for which our souls were hungry. Michael and I tried the little Polish poetry we knew, but it lacked the spirit; somehow Pushkin was more convincing. I don't remember the words, but I can still feel the beat. Our stomachs were empty; we were skin and bones; but hopeful words sometimes meant more than food. That and the few rays of April sun were two things the Nazis could not take away from us.

Soon afterward Michael came down with an infection and a high fever. Ilya tried to doctor him, and I did whatever I could.

In spite of our efforts he was taken away to sick bay, from which no one ever returned. We felt perfectly helpless; nonetheless, Ilya believed that by some miracle Michael would come out alive. He spoke of the power of spring and the beginning of life. I thought that he was romanticizing and told him so. He kept insisting that Michael had a good chance of surviving.

A week went by, and one morning, shortly before we were about to leave for the factory, I noticed several trucks lined up outside our barrack. The sick were being loaded into the trucks by orderlies. At the tailgate of the last truck sat Michael, wrapped in a torn blanket. His eyes were closed.

I ran inside the barrack, found Ilya, and pulled him quickly toward the door so he could see Michael. Without saying a word we went outside, walked over to the truck, and ascertained that no guard was in sight. Ilya and I instinctively reached up and pulled Michael to the ground. We were alone in a narrow area between the barrack and the truck. We tied the blanket around Michael, turned him on his side, and told him to roll as far as possible under the barrack. The barrack stood on stilts, and there was enough room to hide. "Michael, stay under there until we come back to get you," I told him. In a weak voice he answered, "I understand." We ran back before the other prisoners emerged from their barracks; soon we would form columns of five and march off to board the cattle train that would take us to the factory in St. Georgen. Michael rolled away and disappeared behind some cement blocks supporting the middle of the barrack. There was a slight depression in the ground, and he rolled right into it.

We hoped that no one would find him there. When we got back to camp that evening it was still light. We decided to wait until dark before getting Michael out of his hiding place. We would have to bring him inside the barrack without anybody noticing him, and we would have to do so quickly. Ilya and I had managed to save some extra bread for Michael; we knew how hungry he must be. Before long dusk fell, and soon it was dark enough for me to slip under the barrack and crawl close to Michael. He didn't move; I thought he was asleep. I tapped him on the shoulder, and he opened his eyes. I motioned to him that he could come out now. We had to be cautious; the camp was overrun with SS men and *kapos*. Ilya coughed twice to let us know all was clear, and we crawled out. We managed to get Michael into a prisoner's uniform taken from a dead inmate; we even found him a hat and a pair of wooden clogs. We sneaked him into the barrack and put him into an empty bunk next to a friend of Ilya's. Incredibly, no one paid any attention; in the commotion of hundreds of people forming a supper line and groups of "traders" combing the barrack, nobody saw us bring him inside.

Our scheme worked, and Michael was not discovered. He managed to stay in the barrack, hidden underneath a bunk during the day and sleeping in the empty bunk at night. During the day our night-shift friends took care of him. Michael wasn't getting any better, but he was still alive, and we kept him going. One week after his arrival, at the end of April, we stopped going out to the factory. On May 5, 1945, we were liberated with the help of three American tanks, and Michael was taken to the Mauthausen hospital by U.S. army medics. Ilya returned to Russia to look for his family, and I went to look for my family in Poland. Before we parted Ilya confessed to me that he was a Jew, but that he had had to keep it a secret while a prisoner of the Nazis. For medical reasons he was never circumcised, he told me, and that was what had saved him from being discovered. Even his Russian friends didn't know it. He was light, he had gray eyes, and he looked like a typical Slav. He would have been shot had the Nazis known him to be a Jew. It was an emotional farewell, and with it Ilya and I parted.

On May 4, 1946, a day short of one year later, I ran into Michael walking down a street in Paris. We had gained weight, our hair had grown in, we were fairly well dressed, and it took us a moment to recognize each other. Once we overcame the initial shock we found a little bistro and decided to celebrate.

It was almost the first anniversary of our liberation, and it was hard to believe that such accidental meetings were possible, never mind so appropriately timed.

Michael talked about his deliverance and assured me that he would never forget what Ilya and I had done for him. I assured him that he would have done the same thing had the roles been reversed. "I don't think so," he answered. "I'm a coward at heart." I wasn't sure if I was any different; suddenly it occurred to me that if I had known the consequences of pulling Michael from the truck at the time, I might not have done it either. It had been done on impulse, of that I was sure. I never pretended it to be a heroic act. I knew only that it was a risk.

Michael had found two of his siblings, and they were all getting ready to emigrate to Latin America. He swore, of course, to keep in touch.

One year later I came to America; in the excitement of the move I temporarily forgot about Michael. The same thing must have happened to him. I did not hear from or about him until twenty years later; in 1966, by chance, I met a mutual friend who gave me Michael's address. I wrote him immediately. Some weeks later I received an answer. I was very excited opening the envelope. After twenty years, I thought, Michael and I had made contact again! The letter read:

Dear Sir,
   If you could only refresh my memory and tell me where and when we met. For the love of God, I can't remember anybody with a name such as yours.